D1569055

The Emden-Ayesha Adventure

CLASSICS OF NAVAL LITERATURE

JACK SWEETMAN, SERIES EDITOR

This series makes available new editions of classic works of naval history, biography, and fiction. Each volume is complete and unabridged and includes an authoritative introduction written specifically for the Naval Institute Press. A list of titles published or currently in preparation appears at the end of this volume.

The Emden-Ayesha Adventure

German Raiders in the South Seas and Beyond, 1914

Hellmuth von Mücke

Translated by
J. H. Klein Jr.

With an introduction by
Terrell D. Gottschall

NAVAL INSTITUTE PRESS
Annapolis, Maryland

Naval Institute Press
291 Wood Road
Annapolis, MD 21402

Library of Congress Cataloging-in-Publication Data

Mücke, Hellmuth von, b. 1881.
    [Emden. English]
    The Emden-Ayesha adventure : German raiders in the South Seas
and beyond, 1914 / Hellmuth von Mücke ; translated by J. H. Klein Jr.;
with an introduction by Terrell D. Gottschall.
        p. cm.—(Classics of naval literature)
    Translation of Emden and Ayesha originally published in the
Proceedings of the U.S. Naval Institute 1916 and 1917.
    ISBN 1-55750-873-9 (alk. paper)
    1. Emden (Cruiser) 2. Ayesha (Schooner) 3. Germany. Kriegsmarine—
History—World War, 1914–1918. 4. World War, 1914–1918—
Naval operations, German. 5. Mücke, Hellmuth von, b. 1881. 6.
World War, 1914–1918—Personal narratives, German. I. Mücke,
Hellmuth von, b. 1881. Ayesha. English. II. Title: Ayesha. III. Title.
IV. Series.

D582.E6M813 2000
940.4'5943—dc21   00-35162

Printed in the United States of America on acid-free
paper ⊚

07 06 05 04 03 02 01 00   9 8 7 6 5 4 3 2
First printing

All photographs are from the Imperial War Museum.

Contents

Introduction

The Emden-Ayesha Adventure is an epic story that could be fiction but is, in reality, fact. It describes the adventures of a unit, commanded by Kapitänleutnant (Lieutenant Commander) Hellmuth von Mücke, detached from the German raider *Emden* during the early months of World War I. Mücke and his fifty-man detachment landed on Direction Island, in the Indian Ocean, on 9 November 1914 with orders to destroy British radio and cable facilities. While Mücke and his men were ashore, SMS *Emden* steamed away to fight a losing battle with HMAS *Sydney*. To avoid capture, the landing detachment seized the *Ayesha*, a small three-masted schooner, and escaped to sea. This began a seven-month odyssey that took Mücke and his crew by schooner and steamer, zambuk, and camel from Direction Island to Constantinople. The tale is an exciting one as Mücke and his men survive equinoctial storms in the Indian Ocean, slip through the Allied blockade in the Red Sea, and fight their way through hostile Bedouins in Arabia.

Mücke's story succeeds as both a rousing tale of adventure and a subtle comment on wartime literature.[1] Originally published soon after his return to Germany in 1915, this light-hearted but quietly patriotic book would have provided German readers with a small but satisfying propaganda coup after the loss of the *Emden* and other recent naval defeats. English-language editions, with their heroic portrayal of chivalric seamen, momentarily countered the negative image of the German Navy caused by the adoption of unrestricted submarine warfare.[2] (This Classics of Naval Literature edition, translated by an American naval officer, was serialized in the U.S. Naval Institute *Proceedings* in 1916 and 1917.) Mücke does not beat the angry drum of nationalism so common at the time. Instead, he paints his foes in fairly positive tones, reserving criticism only for the British press, which announced the "sinking" of the *Emden* on numerous occasions; the neutral Dutch, who threatened to intern the *Ayesha*'s crew in the East Indies; the Bedouins who attacked his column in the deserts of Arabia; and the Turks, from whom he received little allied cooperation.

Although the story's basic facts reflect Mücke's official reports, he adds a personal touch that elevates the account to epic level. His constant theme is courage in the face of adversity. He admires the *Emden*'s captain, Commander Karl von Müller, whose chivalry earned him the sobriquet of the "last gentleman of war" even from his opponents.[3] Mücke himself writes proudly of his crew's stoic courage as they overcome danger and hardship with an unflappable manner. The *Ayesha*'s crew survive the lack of creature comforts—razor blades, tobacco, toothbrushes—with the same calm strength and equanimity that sees them through a desert ambush in Arabia. Mücke writes with a wry sense of humor. He notes that the *Emden*'s crew were unable to replace their uniforms.

> The trousers, which were originally of the regular length, gradually came through at the calf and then at the knee. After a time the long trousers became short ones, a little later the short ones became bathing trunks, and again a little later—

of this, I will not tell! I need only remark that the uncovered
parts were soon hidden by coal dust. (p. 57)

At one point he notes his difficulty in hiring a native pilot
in East Indies waters due to a lack of funds. He possesses only
a shilling and twopence, confiscated from the *Ayesha*'s original
crew as "war treasure for the Imperial Treasury." When later
confronted by a Dutch warship with the possibility that
Dutch authorities might intern the unarmed *Ayesha* and its
crew, Mücke jokingly warns the Dutch commander, "I hope
we two will not have an engagement when I leave again"
(p. 116).

   Though Mücke's story may never rise to the level of the
classical epic, it nonetheless shares common features with
some examples of the genre. The detachment's determination
to return home compares in some ways to Homer's *Odyssey* as
Odysseus spends ten years attempting to return to Ithaca following the Trojan War. The battle in the desert suggests the
"March of the Ten Thousand" as Xenophon leads a Greek
army on a fighting retreat out of the interior of Persia in his
Anabasis. The cruise of the *Ayesha* resembles Lieutenant William Bligh's journal describing his voyage in an open boat
from Tahiti to Timor following the mutiny on HMS *Bounty*.
Mücke's tale even evokes the sense of contemporary adventure
novelists such as John Buchan, who describes a thrilling chase
along the Danube and into eastern Turkey during the early
days of World War I in *Greenmantle*; H. Rider Haggard and
his Allan Quartermain series; or Erskine Childer's seminal es-
pionage novel, *The Riddle of the Sands*.

Hellmuth Karl von Mücke was born on 26 June 1881 in
Zwickau, Saxony. His father was an Army officer who later
transferred to the imperial civil service. Mücke entered the
Imperial German Navy as a cadet in April 1900. He received
his commission as *Leutnant zur See* (Lieutenant, j.g.) in September 1903 and was immediately detailed as a watch officer

aboard SMS *Nymphe* (3,000 tons, ten 105mm guns), a modern light cruiser that had just joined the fleet. For the next decade, he served in a series of sea and staff assignments with the 3d Torpedo Boat Half-Flotilla, Scouting Forces, and the 1st Torpedo Boat Flotilla. He commanded the torpedo boat *S. 149* and, following promotion to lieutenant commander, was posted as an *Admiralstabsoffizier* in Berlin. He joined SMS *Emden* in late 1913 as navigator and became executive officer on the eve of war in June 1914.

Following the arrival of the landing detachment in Constantinople, Mücke returned to Germany in triumph. His published criticism of Germany's Turkish allies and a perceived bent toward self-promotion, however, earned him the disapproval of the Foreign Ministry and fellow officers. He assumed command of the 15th Torpedo Boat Half-Flotilla (*Halbflottille*), an element of the High Seas Fleet, in June 1915. He returned to the Ottoman Empire in early 1916 to command the Euphrates River Detachment in operations against British gunboats in the Mesopotamian campaign. Subsequently he commanded a unit in the Austro-Hungarian Danube Flotilla before joining the battlecruiser *Derfflinger* (31,000 tons, eight 30.5cm guns) as navigator. Mücke formally retired from the Navy on 30 August 1919 with the rank of captain.

Mücke's postwar career was equally colorful. He joined the German Workers Party after demobilization but resigned when Adolf Hitler began to transform it into the Nazi Party in 1921. Mücke's dislike for Hitler's cult of personality and a political critique published in 1931 earned him persecution by the Nazis. He derived a small income from royalties for his works on *Emden* and *Ayesha* and a handful of navigational handbooks. Mücke, who lost a son on the Russian front during World War II, died in 1957.[4]

The Imperial German Navy's presence in Asian waters reflected nearly a century of economic and strategic interest in East Asia. By the first quarter of the nineteenth century, Brit-

ain had secured dominance in India, France had established a
foothold in Indochina, Holland ruled the East Indies, and
Spain controlled the Philippines. These colonial ventures left
only China available to substantial German trade. The first
German merchant ship reached Canton in 1828. German ton-
nage in East Asian waters increased to 500,000 tons by 1864,
and German trade exceeded 20,000,000 marks a decade later.
Eventually, German investment in East Asia became second
only to that of Great Britain.[5]

Compared to other European fleets, the German Navy was
a relative newcomer to Asia and the Pacific. The first German
warships—a small Prussian squadron—reached East Asia in
1860 with orders to protect German trade and initiate diplomatic ties with China and Japan. Count Philip von Eulen-
burg, who had accompanied the squadron, negotiated a treaty
with China in September 1861 on behalf of Prussia and other
German states. The treaty expressly permitted Prussian warships to operate in Chinese waters for the protection of trade
or the suppression of piracy.[6]

Given the importance of Asian trade, the Prussian Navy
decided to create a permanent naval presence with the establishment of a formal East Asian area of operations in 1867.
The boundaries of the new station ranged westward into the
central Indian Ocean, eastward into the western Pacific, and
southward to include the Dutch East Indies and the Philippines. Two sloops and two gunboats formed the standard contingent on station thereafter. The lack of a base, however, soon
inhibited operations on the new station. German warships had
to depend on British (Hong Kong), Chinese (Shanghai), or
Japanese (Nagasaki) facilities for logistical and technical support. Although Prussian ships surveyed several potential base
sites in 1869, the outbreak of the Franco-German War in
1870 deferred a final decision for a generation.[7] Such support
points were nonetheless necessary for overseas operations. As
Alfred Thayer Mahan would write in 1890: "To provide rest-
ing-places for [ships], where they coal and repair, would be

one of the first duties of a government proposing to itself the development of the power of the nation at sea."[8]

The strategic and economic importance of the western Pacific led the new Imperial German Navy to create an even more formal structure in the 1880s. The various ships assigned to the station had originally operated independently of each other. Because this practice eventually undermined operational effectiveness, the navy decided to establish an integrated squadron under the command of a flag officer.[9] Formally established in 1881 under Commodore (later Rear Admiral) Louis von Blanc, the squadron initially consisted of a diverse mix of warships: the steam corvette *Stosch* (3,000 tons, ten 150mm guns), screw frigates *Hertha* (2,500 tons, nineteen 150mm guns) and *Elizabeth* (2,900 tons, seventeen 150mm guns), and gunboats *Wolf* (600 tons, two 125mm guns) and *Iltis* (600 tons, two 125mm guns).[10]

The new unit acted as a flying squadron responding to problems anywhere on the station. The larger ships, eventually designated as cruisers, showed the flag and undertook anti-piracy patrols. The gunboats proved particularly effective for operations in shallow coastal waters and China's river basins. Because German warships did not carry marines, officers and seamen received training as naval infantry, qualifying in small arms and practicing amphibious operations.

The East Asia squadron disappeared in 1884 when Germany needed its ships to support the development of a colonial empire in Africa and the south Pacific. The navy transferred some of its vessels to the Indian Ocean to support the "scramble for Africa." The new unit, now configured as the *Kreuzergeschwader* (Cruiser Squadron), became a powerful and mobile task force responsible for the acquisition of German East Africa, German Southwest Africa, Togoland, and Cameroon.[11]

The sudden appearance of a cruiser was generally enough to enforce the will of an imperial power. Marlow, Joseph Conrad's protagonist in *Heart of Darkness*, notes,

Once, I remember, we came upon a man-of-war anchored off the coast. There wasn't even a shed there, and she was shelling the bush. . . . Her ensign dropped limp like a rag; the muzzles of the long six-inch guns stuck out all over the low hull; the greasy, slimy swell swung her up lazily and let her down, swaying her thin masts. In the empty immensity of earth, sky and water, there she was, incomprehensible, firing into a continent.[12]

For the next few years, the Cruiser Squadron performed multiple missions. Its ships showed the imperial flag in foreign waters, policed Germany's new colonial empire, and protected German nationals. The squadron returned briefly to East Asia in 1891 before continuing across the vast Pacific to San Francisco, California. During the Chilean civil war of 1891, its ships landed a three-hundred-man naval brigade at Valparaiso and joined other international units to restore order in the war-torn city. The squadron then proceeded around Cape Horn and through the Magellan straits to Cape Town to resume patrols in African waters. Following intervention in Zanzibar in 1893, the navy decided to deactivate the squadron and assign its ships to various stations.[13]

The outbreak of the Sino-Japanese War in 1894 revived the need for a larger German naval presence in East Asia. The navy therefore created the four-ship *Kreuzerdivision* (Cruiser Division) in September 1894 and dispatched it to the East Asian station. Emperor William II appointed Rear Admiral Paul Hoffmann to command the new unit with specific orders to explore possible base sites in China.[14]

Hoffmann's command initially consisted of the modern light cruiser *Irene* (5,000 tons, fourteen 150mm guns) and the obsolete steam-sail corvettes *Arcona* (2,700 tons, ten 150mm guns), *Alexandrine* (2,700 tons, ten 150mm guns), and *Marie* (2,400 tons, ten 150mm guns). When the navy soon decided that this small force was insufficient to project German sea power in the region, the heavy cruiser *Kaiser* (8,800 tons, eight

260mm guns) and light cruiser *Prinzess Wilhelm* (5,000 tons, fourteen 150mm) replaced the *Alexandrine* and *Marie*. Hoffmann could also call on the light cruiser *Cormoran* (1,900 tons, eight 105mm guns), which operated independently on the East Asian station.

The primary mission of the new division now became the search for a base in East Asia. Hoffmann and his successors—Rear Admiral Alfred von Tirpitz, 1896–97, and Rear Admiral Otto von Diederichs, 1897–99—surveyed and evaluated potential base sites. On 21 August 1897 Diederichs wrote the pivotal analysis that convinced the emperor and the Naval High Command to accept Kiao-chou Bay on the Shantung Peninsula.[15]

The opportunity to acquire a base for the Cruiser Squadron occurred soon thereafter. When members of a xenophobic Chinese secret society murdered two German Catholic missionaries on 1 November 1897, Diederichs requested and received permission to seize Kiao-chou as compensation. He arrived off Tsingtao, a fishing village at the mouth of Kiao-chou Bay, on 13 November with the heavy cruiser *Kaiser* and light cruisers *Prinzess Wilhelm* and *Cormoran*. The three ships cleared for action but made no other aggressive moves. Instead, Diederichs went ashore to examine Chinese readiness under the guise of a friendly visit. He discovered to his satisfaction that local Chinese garrison—three thousand troops commanded by General Chang Kao-yuan—were completely unaware of an impending German attack and, in any event, unprepared to defend their positions.

Sunday, 14 November, dawned clear and cool with light easterly winds. The *Cormoran* steamed into the inner bay to bring several forts and garrison's powder magazine directly under its 105mm guns. The *Kaiser* and *Prinzess Wilhelm* cleared for action at 0600, manned main batteries, and lowered boats to transport the amphibious force—30 officers, 77 petty officers, and 610 seamen—ashore. The surprise assault was completely successful. The landing detachment occupied all scheduled targets by midmorning. As the *Prinzess Wilhelm* fired a twenty-one-gun salute and a ship's band played "Deutschland über Alles," the naval brigade raised the imperial German flag over Germany's first and only Asian possession.[16]

To protect the new territory, the navy decided to revive the *Kreuzergeschwader*. Diederichs would command the squadron with his existing ships as its 1st Division. The navy then created the 2d Division—heavy cruisers *Deutschland* (8,800 tons, eight 260mm guns) and *Kaiserin Augusta* (6,400 tons, twelve 150mm guns) and the light cruiser *Gefion* (4,200 tons, ten 105mm guns)—under Rear Admiral Prince Henry of Prussia, the emperor's brother. As the reinforcements prepared to leave Germany, William directed his brother to ruthlessly punish resistance to German expansion: "Should anyone seek to hinder you in the proper exercise of our legitimate rights, go for them with a mailed fist!"[17]

The Treaty of Peking, signed on 6 March 1898, granted Germany a ninety-nine-year leasehold (*Pachtgebiet*) of an area fifty kilometers around Kiao-chou Bay. Section I formally permitted the German Navy to develop and fortify a base "for the repair and equipment of her ships" at Tsingtao. Section II granted Germany the right to construct railroads and mine coal within the leasehold and elsewhere in the Shantung peninsula.[18] The coal was particularly valuable to the Cruiser Squadron, which would no longer need to depend on foreign sources.

The navy now began to transform Tsingtao and Kiao-chou into a naval base (*Flottenstützpunkt*) and the new home port of the *Kreuzergeschwader*. Naval engineers designed and developed two large artificial harbors in Kiao-chou Bay with berths for sixty ships, dockyard, dry dock, rail line, machine shop, armory, and chandlery. Other work crews mounted 240mm coastal artillery and 280mm mortars in *Festung Tsingtao*. The fifteen-hundred-man 3d *Seebattalion* (Naval Infantry Battalion) arrived from Germany to provide Tsingtao's garrison. The new base's personnel soon numbered 2,400.[19]

Tsingtao and Kiao-chou quickly became the center of German trade in China. More than nine hundred steamers, with cargoes valued at 7 million pounds, visited Tsingtao in 1913. The leasehold eventually contained eight hundred kilometers of railroad track, providing rail access to Peking and the Yangtze basin, and produced five hundred thousand tons of coal annually by 1914. A combination of good weather, German orderliness, and the Germania Brewery's world-famous "Tsingtao" beer soon made the city a popular vacation spot for Europeans in the Far East.[20]

The *Kreuzergeschwader* next saw action in the Philippines during the Spanish-American War. Rear Admiral George Dewey, commander of the U.S. Asiatic Squadron, had blockaded Manila following his destruction of the Spanish fleet at the Battle of Manila Bay. Diederichs sent light cruisers *Irene* and *Cormoran* to observe the blockade and protect German nationals in May. When Diederichs arrived with the *Kaiserin Augusta, Kaiser*, and *Prinzess Wilhelm* in June, Dewey viewed the German force with suspicion, particularly when a German transport carrying fifteen hundred seamen also entered the bay. This large German presence was innocent enough, however; the German ships had rendezvoused at Manila to simplify the process of transshipment whereby the Germans relieved half of each crew every two years. The presence of several American reporters, imbued with a strong dose of "yellow journalism," aboard Dewey's ships only exacerbated the situation.

The summer grew hot and tense when a series of unintentional confrontations, often involving SMS *Irene*, strained relations between Diederichs and Dewey. The Americans accused the Germans of violating their blockade; the Germans accused the Americans of violating international law. The incident reached a climax in July when Dewey threatened to go to war against the Germans, but an exchange of formal letters and Manila's surrender in August eased the situation.[21]

The *Kreuzergeschwader* acquired a single benefit from the Spanish-American War. When Spain dismantled its overseas empire, Germany purchased the Caroline, Marshall, and Mariana (less Guam) islands in 1899. The navy could not afford to construct any bases in the new colonies but did establish a series of coaling depots.

The *Kreuzergeschwader*, now commanded by Vice Admiral Felix von Bendemann, returned to China in 1900 during the Boxer Rebellion. Fearing that unrest would threaten the fledging base at Tsingtao, the squadron's ships joined an international force to attack the Taku forts that commanded the river approaches to Peking in June. The ships bombarded the forts with their main batteries and then landed naval infantrymen to seize the positions. Another five hundred naval infantrymen joined the expedition that raised the siege of Peking's Legation Quarter in August. Because the incident underlined the strategic importance of East Asia, the navy dispatched the modern heavy cruiser *Fürst Bismarck* (11,500 tons, four 240mm, twelve 150mm guns) to reinforce the Cruiser Squadron.[22]

Once the acquisition of Kiao-chou and the South Sea islands satisfied Germany's imperial aspirations in Asia and the Pacific, the primary purpose of the *Kreuzergeschwader* became commerce raiding (*guerre de course*). Commerce raiding employed cruisers—midsize, fast, well-armed ships—and hit-and-run tactics to strike at an enemy's commercial lifelines and merchant marine. Inferior naval powers had traditionally used commerce raiding to counteract superior enemy naval forces. Even Mahan, who stressed the role of battleships as the means to sea power, recognized the value of cruiser warfare when a belligerent lacked either a battle fleet or the economic ability to construct one. He noted that commerce raiding, which required only the "maintenance of a few swift cruisers," could inflict substantial maritime and material harm and undermine an enemy's civilian morale.[23]

In the 1880s Admiral Theophile Aube, France's Minister of the Marine, had promoted the idea of *guerre de course* by establishing the *Jeune École* (Young School). Aware that the French could not challenge Britain's capital ship superiority without an expensive and provocative naval arms race, Aube adopted the motto "Shamelessly attack the weak, shamelessly flee the strong." Only commerce raiding, he believed, would seriously threaten British dependence on colonial ties and international trade.[24]

The *Jeune École* had a mixed impact on Germany. German naval planners in the 1880s had not yet established a single, unified strategic vision for the Imperial German Navy. For example, the current chief of the Admiralty, General Leo Caprivi, still perceived the navy as little more than an adjunct to the powerful German Army. Senior naval officers themselves could not decide whether to construct battleships as the foundation of a battle fleet (*Geschwaderkrieg*, "squadron war") or cruisers for commerce raiding (*Kreuzerkrieg*, "cruiser war"). This internal debate lasted for more than a decade until Rear Admiral Alfred von Tirpitz convinced Emperor William II in 1897 to adopt a Mahanian battle fleet using battleships concentrated "between Helgoland and the Thames."[25]

Although this new focus on home waters relegated the Cruiser Squadron to a secondary role, the navy nonetheless acknowledged the effectiveness of commerce raiding as the *Kreuzergeschwader*'s primary mission in the event of war with another maritime power. Diederichs, who had returned to Berlin in 1899 as chief of the Admiralty Staff, now assumed responsibility for the direction of ships on foreign service and the development of operational plans (O-Plan). He devised the first O-Plan for the *Kreuzergeschwader* in February 1900. Following the outbreak of war, the Cruiser Squadron would immediately commence commerce raiding: "Das Kreuzergeschwader führt Kreuzerkrieg." Diederichs believed that "cruiser war" in East Asia and the Indian Ocean would require the British to weaken their forces in Atlantic waters in order to protect the British Empire and colonial trade in Asia. The orders directed the cruisers assigned to the East African station to proceed across the Indian Ocean via Diego Garcia and the Cocos Islands to reinforce the *Kreuzergeschwader*.[26]

Diederichs worried that the lack of bases to provide logistical and technical support would hamper operations. He fully understood the principle formulated by Mahan in 1890 that cruisers without bases were like land birds "unable to fly far from their own shores."[27] He complained, "No secure base is yet available. Years will pass before the first one—Kiaochou—can be completed." He therefore proposed the establishment of a network of coaling depots beyond Suez. He designated the Farasan Islands sat the southern end of the Red Sea, Langkawi Island on the west coast of the Malayan Peninsula, and We Island on the north coast of Sumatra as potential sites.[28]

In addition to these coaling depots, Diederichs recommended the assignment of agents (*Vertrauensmänner*), either trustworthy civilians or reserve officers, to neutral ports. These agents would purchase coal and provisions, charter steamers, and organize rendezvous sites to provide additional support for the Cruiser Squadron. Because coal was the most important issue for the *Kreuzergeschwader*, he also planned to preposition colliers at various sites throughout the station once war broke out. In addition, the squadron commander was responsible for acquiring additional colliers or tenders for each of his ships.[29]

Diederichs proposed the reinforcement of the Cruiser Squadron in his operational orders for 1902. Although the modern heavy cruiser *Fürst Bismarck* had recently replaced the obsolete *Kaiser*, Germany still had only the sixth largest naval contingent in East Asia. He believed that additional ships were necessary if the squadron were to carry out its mission effectively. He also ordered the squadron to implement commerce raiding—"Shamelessly attack the weak"—but avoid open battle with the superior British forces—"Shamelessly flee the strong"—except in conjunction with Germany's Triple Alliance partners (Austria-Hungary and Italy).[30]

The Cruiser Squadron's O-Plans changed only slightly during the next decade. Rear Admiral Wilhelm von Büchsel, Diederichs's successor as head of the Admiralty Staff, proposed a direct attack by the Cruiser Squadron on the West Coast of the United States in plans developed between 1903 and 1905. The purpose of the plan was to prevent the dispatch of U.S. warships to the Philippines or the Atlantic. The growing strength of the U.S. Pacific Fleet, however, eventually forced the Cruiser Squadron to focus on commerce raiding against American merchant ships combined with hit-and-run raids on Guam and the Philippines. Büchsel also concluded that British naval superiority would inhibit the effectiveness of commerce raiding in the Indian Ocean and western Pacific. He therefore proposed in 1904 that the Cruiser Squadron turn east to interdict the shipping lanes between Vancouver, British Columbia, and East Asia. By 1906 the development of closer Anglo-Japanese ties caused another revision, which once again focused the Cruiser Squadron's attention on the Indian Ocean and Australian waters, with operations to range as far west as East Africa. Japanese naval superiority prompted later O-Plans to give the *Kreuzergeschwader*'s commander the latitude to leave Asian waters and operate elsewhere if necessary. When the arrival on station of the modern heavy cruisers *Scharnhorst* and *Gneisenau* (13,000 tons, eight 210mm) in 1909 and 1910 gave the Cruiser Squadron a strong offensive core, plans developed in 1913 and repeated in 1914 confirmed commerce raiding as first priority but established the defeat in detail of British forces as a secondary goal.[31]

When the Great War broke out with the "guns of August" in 1914, the squadron immediately implemented its operational plans. Commander Karl von Müller, commanding officer of SMS *Emden,* had already proceeded to sea in anticipation of the coming of war. Constructed at the Imperial Dockyard, Danzig, the light cruiser *Emden* was commissioned on 10 July 1910 and immediately assigned to the *Kreuzergeschwader* for service in East Asia. The *Emden* was ideal for commerce raiding. The ship displaced 4,300 tons and carried a primary battery of ten 105cm guns. Two sets of Parsons turbines plus two three-cylinder triple-expansion engines propelled the ship at a flank speed of 24 knots. The *Emden*'s coal bunkers, however, contained only 790 tons of coal, which restricted its range to 3,700 nautical miles at a 12-knot cruising speed.[32] The *Emden*'s graceful lines and white paint, as Mücke noted, truly earned it the epithet "Swan of the East" (p. 59).

The *Emden* drew first blood on 4 August, seizing the Russian mail steamer *Ryazan* (3,500 tons).[33] Accompanied by the tender *Markomannia*, the *Emden* then proceeded south to rendezvous with the other ships of the Cruiser Squadron—heavy cruisers *Scharnhorst* and *Gneisenau* and light cruisers *Nürnberg, Leipzig*, and *Dresden*—at Pagan in the Mariana Islands.

Vice Admiral Maximilian Graf von Spee, the squadron's able and aggressive commander, convened a meeting of his senior officers aboard the flagship *Scharnhorst* on the thirteenth to decide how to proceed. The lack of bases, meaning no ready access to coal and technical support, now bore bitter fruit. Spee concluded that his squadron could not operate effectively in the western Pacific or Indian Ocean, where superior enemy forces and inadequate supplies of coal would hinder his movements. He therefore decided to proceed to the west coast of South America, a target-rich region where coal would be more readily available. Captain Müller convinced Spee to leave the *Emden* behind to operate independently. As the newest and fastest of the squadron's light cruisers, it could wreak havoc in the shipping lanes of the Indian Ocean, fulfilling the squadron's war plan for commerce raiding. The *Emden* and the Cruiser Squadron parted company on 14 August 1914 as Müller set a westward course and Spee disappeared into the vast reaches of the Pacific.

The *Emden* never rejoined the *Kreuzergeschwader*. Pursued by Japanese and British forces, Spee reappeared off the coast of Chile in October. His ships collided with a small British squadron, consisting of older and slower warships, near Cape Coronel, Chile, at dusk on 1 November. Sent from the Atlantic to intercept Spee, Rear Admiral Sir Christopher Cradock commanded the armored cruisers *Good Hope* (14,100 tons, two 9.2-inch and sixteen 6-inch guns) and *Monmouth* (9,800 tons, fourteen 6-inch guns) and the light cruiser *Glasgow* (4,800 tons, two 6-inch and ten 4-inch guns). In the ensuing battle, *Good Hope* and *Monmouth* were sunk with no survivors. Spee's ships escaped largely unscathed to proceed through the Straits of Magellan into the South Atlantic.

Spee now decided to raid the British facilities, which he anticipated would be largely undefended, at the Falkland Islands before proceeding north. When the German ships arrived off Port Stanley early on the morning of 8 December, they discovered instead a powerful British squadron consisting of two battlecruisers and three heavy cruisers plus the light cruiser *Glasgow*. The battlecruisers (*Invincible* and *Inflexible*), designed to hunt down and destroy cruisers like Spee's, displaced 17,000 tons and carried 12-inch guns. The ensuing Battle of the Falklands was the reciprocal of Coronel. The *Dresden* alone escaped; *Scharnhorst, Gneisenau, Leipzig,* and *Nürnberg* were sunk after a long stern chase. Only 215 of the cruisers' 2,200 crewmen survived. Only ten British sailors were killed.[34]

The fate of the German naval base at Tsingtao was equally tragic. Japanese forces, supported by token British and Indian troops, landed nearby in September and besieged the German positions. Although Tsingtao's only remaining warship, the torpedo boat *S 90* (400 tons, three 450mm torpedo tubes), torpedoed and sank the aging Japanese cruiser *Takachiho* on 17 October, the outnumbered German garrison surrendered on 7 November 1914.[35]

Left behind by Spee and cut off from Tsingtao, the *Emden*

now accomplished the single most successful surface raider cruise of World War I. During the four months from 1 August to 9 November 1914, it captured or sank fifteen merchant ships with a combined displacement of 66,000 tons. Müller took his ship into Madras harbor on 22 September on a daring nighttime raid, causing light but sensational damage to local fortifications and oil tanks. On 28 October the *Emden* raided Penang, Malaya, sinking the Russian light cruiser *Jemtchug* (3,100 tons, six 127mm guns) and the French torpedo-boat destroyer *Mousquet* (300 tons, one 65mm and six 47mm guns). Müller was careful to avoid causing unnecessary casualties during these actions. For example, even though other warships had begun to pursue the *Emden* out of Penang harbor, Müller stopped to rescue thirty-five officers and men from the sinking French ship.[36] The *Emden* also fulfilled another important objective of commerce raiding: tying up enemy naval assets. Mücke notes that at one time sixteen Allied cruisers were chasing the *Emden* (pp. 30, 39, and 44).

The *Emden*'s cruise eventually took it deep into the Indian Ocean near the vicinity of the Cocos (Keeling) Islands by November. Müller decided to land a small detachment on Direction Island to destroy British radio and telegraph facilities. He assigned the mission to his executive officer, Lieutenant Hellmuth von Mücke. The landing detachment consisted of three officers and forty-seven enlisted men armed with the *Emden*'s four 8mm machine guns, twenty-nine Mauser rifles, and twenty-four revolvers. Unbeknownst to Müller, a convoy of Australian troopships escorted by several light cruisers was only a few miles away, in position to receive the panicked message transmitted by the Direction Island station. The ensuring arrival of HMAS *Sydney* (5,400 tons, eight 6-inch guns) caught both Müller and Mücke by surprise. In the ensuing battle, the *Sydney* had advantages both in speed and weaponry. Even though the *Emden* made several gallant torpedo attacks, the ultimate outcome was never in doubt. To save the surviving members of his crew, Müller beached the ship on North

Keeling Island and hoisted a white flag. The *Emden* lost 135 killed and 60 wounded; the *Sydney*, only three killed and eight wounded.[37]

As the *Emden* hauled off to fight the *Sydney*, Mücke made plans to escape the island in case the enemy won the battle. His after-action report noted succinctly, "The landing detachment was unable to rejoin *Emden*." He therefore decided to seize the schooner *Ayesha*, displacing 97 tons with crew spaces for five, and set sail for the neutral Dutch East Indies. The *Ayesha* survived bad weather and poor charts to arrive at Padang, Sumatra, on 27 November. When Dutch authorities threatened to seize the *Ayesha* and intern its crew, Mücke protested on the grounds that the vessel was a warship (*Kriegsschiff*) and therefore entitled to remain in port unhindered for twenty-four hours.[38] The Dutch authorities belatedly agreed but ordered Mücke to leave before he had a chance to purchase provisions and supplies. As he prepared to proceed to sea, however, German merchant ships in the harbor quickly provided some basic supplies.[39]

Before his departure from Padang, Mücke and the local German consul had arranged a rendezvous with the *Choising*, one of the *Kreuzergeschwader*'s tenders. The two ships rendezvoused at sea on 14 December. Mücke and his crew boarded the *Choising*, a small North German Lloyd liner displacing 1,700 tons, on the fifteenth and, in a sad ceremony, scuttled the *Ayesha*. The *Choising*, in no better shape than the leaking *Ayesha*, carried Mücke northwest through the Indian Ocean to the Red Sea, dodging British and French patrols, disguised in neutral colors and design. Mücke had hoped to rendezvous with SMS *Königsberg*, but that light cruiser was blockaded on the African coast by British forces. The *Choising* therefore turned north to disembark the detachment on Turkish territory at Hodeida (Yemen) on 8 January 1915.[40]

Mücke and his crew then began the longest and most dangerous stage of their trek. Sometimes by land, sometimes by sea, they traveled north up the coast of Arabia, dodging more

British and French patrols and fighting Bedouin tribesmen.
They finally arrived at Jiddah, the terminal of the Hejaz railroad, in May. Accompanied by German diplomatic represen-
tatives and reporters, Mücke and his detachment made a triumphal journey to Constantinople by rail.[41] Arrayed in new
uniforms and carrying a tattered battle flag from the *Emden*,
the detachment marched past Vice Admiral Wilhelm Souchon
on 23 May 1915. Mücke announced his arrival with the ritual,
"I respectfully report the return of the *Emden*'s landing force
consisting of five officers, seven petty officers and 37 men"
(p. 184).

Terrell D. Gottschall

Notes

1. Hellmuth von Mücke, *Emden-Ayesha* (Berlin: A. Scherl, 1915).
2. The first American edition, *The "Ayesha," being the Adventures of the Landing Squad of the "Emden"* (Boston: Ritter), appeared in 1916.
3. See, for example, R. K. Lochner, *The Last Gentleman of War: The Raider Exploits of the "Emden"* (Annapolis, Md.: Naval Institute Press, 1988).
4. *Ehrenrangliste der Kaiserliche Deutschen Marine, 1914–1918* (Berlin: E. S. Mittler, 1930), 195; "Hellmuth Karl von Mücke," in WWI Biographical Dictionary, The World War I Document Archives, accessed 31 August 1999, <http://raven.cc.ukans.edu/~kansite/ww_one/bio/m/muecke.html>. Mücke's political treatise is *Linie: Rückblicke persönlicher und politischer Art auf das letzte Jahrzwölft der Republik* (Beuern, Hesse: Edelgarten Verlag, 1931). He had intended to write a trilogy—titled *Revolution, Nationalsozialismus und Bürgertum*—but the poor reception of his first volume dissuaded him from continuing.
5. Willi Boelcke, *So kam das Meer zu uns: Die preussisch-deutsche Kriegsmarine in übersee*, 1822–1914 (Frankfurt: Ullstein, 1981), 236–38.
6. The treaty is in *Die Preussische Expedition nach Ost-Asien*, 4 vols. (Berlin: Decker, 1864–73), 4:353–68.
7. Plan zur Erwerbung der Preussische Kriegsmarine von 1865, in RM 1/1849, Bundesarchiv-Militärarchiv (hereafter BAMA), Freiburg. The Prussian Navy also established operational stations in African waters, the Mediterranean, the Caribbean, and the west coast of the American hemisphere.
8. Alfred Thayer Mahan, *The Influence of Sea Power upon History, 1660–1783* (Boston: Little Brown, 1890), 83.
9. Promemoria, 10 May 1880, in RM 1/2385, BAMA, Freiburg.

10. *Rangliste der Kaiserlichen Marine für 1882* (Berlin: Mittler und Sohn, 1881), 106. For ship details, see Erich Gröner, *German Warships, 1815–1945*, vol. 1: *Major Surface Vessels*, revised and expanded by Dieter Jung and Martin Maass (Annapolis, Md.: Naval Institute Press, 1990).

11. Eberhard von Mantey, *Deutsche Marinegeschichte* (Charlottenburg: Verlag "Offene Worte," 1926), 136–45; Boelcke, *So kam das Meer*, 196–224.

12. Joseph Conrad, *Heart of Darkness* (New York: W. W. Norton, 1971), 14.

13. Mantey, *Marinegeschichte*, 175–76.

14 Allerhöchste Kabinetts Ordre, 25 September 1894, in RM 3/6692, BAMA, Freiburg.

15. Diederichs to Knorr, Militär-politische Bericht über die Lage in China und Korea, 21 August 1897, in RM 3/6694, BAMA, Freiburg.

16. Die Besetzung Tsingtao, 14 November 1897, in Nachlass Diederichs, NL 255/24, BAMA, Freiburg.

17. William II, *Die Reden Kaiser Wilhelms II*, edited by Johann Penzler (Leipzig: Philip Reclam, 1904), 2:80.

18. "Convention respecting the lease of Kiaochow," 6 March 1898, in John MacMurray, ed., *Treaties and Agreements with and Concerning China, 1894–1919* (New York: Oxford University Press, 1921), 4:112–16.

19. For the development of Tsingtao as a naval base, see Jork Artelt, *Tsingtau: Deutsche Stadt und Festung in China, 1897–1914* (Düsseldorf: Droste Verlag, 1984), and Joachim Schultz-Naumann, *Unter Kaisers Flagge: Deutschlands Schutzgebiete im Pazifik und in China* (Munich: Universitas Verlag, 1985).

20. Great Britain, Foreign Office, *Kiaochow and Weihaiwei* (London: H.M. Stationery Office, 1920), 1–41.

21. See, particularly, George Dewey, *The Autobiography of George Dewey, Admiral of the Navy* (New York: Charles Scribner's Sons, 1916); Otto von Diederichs, "A Statement of Events in Manila, May–October 1898," *Journal of the Royal United Services Institution*, 59 (1914): 421–46; Hugo von Pohl, "Die Tätigkeit SMS *Irene* in den Gewässern der Philippinen, 1896–1899," *Marine Rundschau* 7 (1902): 759–66.

22. Hans Jürgen Witthöft, *Lexikon zur deutschen Marinegeschichte* (Herford: Koehlers Verlagsgesellschaft, 1977), 1:41–42.

23. Mahan, *Sea Power*, 132.

24. Theodore Ropp, *The Development of a Modern Navy: French Naval Policy, 1871–1904*. Annapolis, Md.: Naval Institute Press, 1987), 155–80; Volkmar Bueb, *Die "Junge Schule" der französischen Marine: Strategie und Politik, 1875–1900* (Boppard am Rhein: Harald Boldt Verlag, 1971), 25–54.

25. For the cruiser-battleship debate, see Jonathan Steinberg, *Yesterday's Deterrent: Tirpitz and the Birth of the German Battle Fleet* (New York: Macmillan, 1965); Volker R. Berghahn, *Der Tirpitz-Plan: Genesis und Verfall einer innen-politischen Krisenstrategie unter Wilhelm II* (Düsseldorf: Droste Verlag, 1971); Hans Hollmann, *Krügerdepesche und Flottenfrage* (Stuttgart: Kohlhammer Verlag, 1927); and Ivo Lambi, *The Navy and German Power Politics, 1862–1914* (Boston: Allen & Unwin, 1984).

26. Operationsbefehle für das Kreuzergeschwader und S. M. Schiffe im Auslande, 1 February 1900, in RM 38/125, BAMA, Freiburg.

27. Mahan, *Sea Power*, 83.

28. Diederichs, Immediatvortrag, 3 February 1900, in RM 5/875, BAMA, Freiburg.

29. Erläuterungen und Ausführungsbestimmungen zu den Allerhöchst genehmigten Operationsbefehlen von 1st Februar 1900, in RM 38/125, BAMA, Freiburg.

30. Diederichs, Immediatvortrag, 8 February 1902, in RM 5/883, BAMA, Freiburg.

31. Ivo Lambi, *Navy and German Power Politics*, 231–35, 408–11; Peter Overlack, "German War Plans in the Pacific, 1900–1914," *The Historian* (1998), 579–93.

32. Gröner, *Major German Warships*, 105–6.

33. The naval base at Tsingtao converted the *Ryazan* into an auxiliary merchant cruiser armed with eight 105mm guns fitted from the obsolete cruiser *Cormoran*. Renamed *Cormoran II*, the ship had a brief and unsuccessful career as a commerce raider before internment by American authorities at Guam in December 1914; see John Walter, *The Kaiser's Pirates: German Surface Raiders in World War I* (Annapolis, Md.: Naval Institute Press, 1994), 183.

34. See particularly Paul G. Halpern, *A Naval History of World War I* (Annapolis, Md.: Naval Institute Press, 1994), 70–100; and Keith Yates, *Graf Spee's Raiders: Challenge to the Royal Navy, 1914–1915* (Annapolis, Md.: Naval Institute Press, 1995).

35. See Charles Burdick, *The Japanese Siege of Tsingtau* (Hamden, Conn.: Archon Books, 1976).

36. See an undated chronological account of SMS *Emden*'s cruise, in RM 99/605, BAMA, Freiburg. For ship details, see Robert Gardiner, ed., *Conway's All the World's Fighting Ships, 1860–1905* (London: Conway Maritime Press, 1997), 326.

37. Yates, *Raiders*, 147–72.

38. Mücke to German consul, Padang, 28 November 1914, RM 99/605, BAMA, Freiburg. Mücke wrote the letter while aboard SS *Kleist* and sent it via the senior officer present of the Royal Dutch Navy.

39. Mücke to Admiralstab, 28 November 1914, in RM 99/605, BAMA, Freiburg.

40. Kriegstagebuch des Landungszuges SMS *Emden*: Keeling-Padang-Perim, 7 January 1915, ibid.

41. Mitteilung des Kapitänleutnant von Mücke über seine Erlebnisse in Arabien, 25 May 1915, ibid.

The Emden-Ayesha Adventure

CHAPTER I

The First Prize

"ALL HANDS ON THE QUARTERDECK" was piped by the boatswain's mates throughout the ship. Soon the entire crew was assembled on the quarterdeck. And each man knew what was coming.

About 2 P.M., August 2, 1914, while cruising in the middle of the Yellow Sea, Commander von Müller appeared on the poop, holding in his hand a telegram such as we used for radio reports. Six hundred eyes eagerly watched the lips of the captain, as he began:

"A radio has been received from Tsingtao as follows: 'His Majesty, the Kaiser, has, on August 1, ordered the mobilization of the entire army and navy. Following an invasion of German territory by Russian troops, the Empire now finds itself embroiled in war with Russia and France.'

"What had been expected for years has now actually occurred. Without making a formal declaration of war the enemy hordes have invaded Germany.

"The German sword has remained sheathed for 44 years, even though in that period we had many favorable opportunities to conquer. But Germany has never striven for conquest by violence. In peaceful rivalry, by industry and work, by trading and commercial efforts, by lofty ideals and culture, by honesty and thoroughness, it has won itself a position of honor among nations. And this is begrudged us by those who could not do likewise. This envy, strengthened by the knowledge of their own inabilities and their endeavors to excel the success of Germany's peaceful pursuits, in education and training, in technique and science, in short, in all the high standards of its civilization and culture, this envy has now moved them to unleash the furies of war and to dare to trust to the sword to solve the problem which was beyond their mental and moral capacities. It is now our duty to show that the German nation, sound to the very core, can also survive this test.

"The war will not be an easy one. For years our enemies have been preparing. 'To exist' or 'not to exist' must be our watchword. We will prove ourselves worthy of our ancestors and forefathers and resist to the end, even though the entire world rise against us.

"I intend first of all to make an attack in the direction of Vladivostok. 'Commerce destruction' is our principal rôle. To the best of our knowledge, the Russian and French men-of-war are gathered near Vladivostok. Therefore, it is quite likely that we may fall in with them. In that case I know that I can safely rely on my entire crew."

Three cheers for H.M. the Kaiser resounded over the broad surface of the Yellow Sea. Then followed the order, "Clear ship for action," all hands going to their posts.

And so we were at war. The "cry for revenge" from the west that has not ceased for decades; the cry that grew especially loud since Germany dared to reannex the ancient Germanic territory that had been snatched away from her by the French pirates during the 200 years of weakness and rebellion, this "revenge cry" has done its work. The bronze die is cast. But this time it is not because of Alsace-Lorraine. Now there is more at stake. First of all, only France and Russia had to be considered. But for many long years it gradually became apparent that behind these stood a third nation, the enemy of all, that for centuries had spilled the warm red blood of all other nations for her own interests: England. After forcing France to her knees in the middle 90's at Fashoda, and humbling her to the very dust because she dared cross England's plans for colonizing Africa, and, after permitting Japan in 1904 to strike a blow at Russia who was becoming uncomfortable in the Far East, she then directed the minds and thoughts of these two now no longer rivals, to seeking in some other quarter that compensation which English greed of power and money denied them in Africa and in East Asia. The humbled France and the defeated Russia must now be used to serve her to attempt to whip Germany. The youthful strength of the German Empire is her most irksome competitor. She could not peaceably compete with our knowledge and technique, our commercial and industrial abilities. Step by step all over the world the Union Jack had to retreat before the colors of our Empire. Peaceful competition does not exist in England. The poisonous slander against Germany which she spread over the telegraphs and cables of the world did not have the desired effect. England's moneybag was in danger. Hence the old principle: "Sink, burn, destroy." She had not yet decided how she would accomplish this. Should she, following her ancient custom, embroil the others in war so that, in the meantime, she could have a free hand in stirring up trouble? Or should she herself take part in the war, fearing that the strength of her credulous and dazzled victims alone was not sufficient to attain for her the goal she wished? England had no well-founded reason for declaring war on us. But, as the saying of these island-folk goes, "that made no difference." They are never at a loss for an excuse whenever one becomes necessary. Justice and law are then treated with indifference, and a hypocritical cloak is always to be found under which to hide her dealings.

What did the famous English statesman, Lord Derby, say in Parliament in the middle of the 19th century in regard to

his own people? He said: "We treat friendly nations shame-
fully. We insist upon the full meaning of international law,
when it suits our purpose; at other times we shrink away from
the provisions of this law. The story of 'The Rights of the
Sea,' which I would like to call 'The Wrongs of the Sea,' is
an indelible sign of the unbridled egoism and the covetousness
of the English nation and its laws."

So much for Lord Derby.

All nations of the earth have felt proofs of England's covetousness and unbridled egoism. One thinks of Spain, whose
growing commercial and colonial power was destroyed by the
English sword, still enduring the thorn in its side—Gibral-
tar—which it had to surrender. One thinks of Holland, whose
riches were despoiled by the blood-sucking English, who still
has England to thank for changing her former grandeur and
power to her present comparative insignificance, one thinks of
Denmark, whose fleet was surprised and sunk in the middle
of peace in 1807, and whose principal city, bombarded by
English guns, was set afire while nobody was thinking of war,
one thinks of China that had a war thrust upon her in 1840
because she was struggling against the English bartering of
opium, one thinks of Egypt, that was stolen from Turkey and
is now constrained to buy its bread at a high price from England in order to swell her income, because England found it
profitable to discourage the cultivation of cereals in the fertile
wheatfields and to substitute cotton therefor in order to be
independent of America in this respect, one thinks of India
where pestilence and famine and the payment of a yearly trib-
ute of one and one-half milliards are the blessings of English
culture, against which the downtrodden and impoverished
people are vainly struggling, one thinks of the Boer states,
which became slaves to England, because they possessed gold
veins and diamond mines, one thinks of Turkey, whose territory England has been dividing up for a long time, of France,
who suffered the humility at Fashoda, of Russia, having Japan

set at her throat, of Portugal, that is merely a vassal of England, of Italy, who is not permitted to expand in Africa, of America (U.S.), whom England tried to forbid the construction and fortification of the Panama Canal, the reasons being known to the whole world only through English sources and according to the English point of view. Having lost her political power over America, in accordance with her old principle, "Ignorance is the proper power to use in combating spirits and nations," she surrounded the "free people" with such clouds of lies sent over her cables that the Americans no longer may even think in "American," but must now think only in "English." In regard to thinking and judging, Americans are bound by the same English slavish yoke that England forced, by the sword, upon all other political powers. And what was it that the Englishman Thomas Carlyle said about the English love of truth? He said: "No Englishman will longer trust the truth. For 200 years he has been hemmed in by lies of all kinds. He considers the plain truth to be dangerous, so he endeavors to modify it (truth) by accompanying it with lies, and yoking the two together. That is what he calls 'adopting the safe middle course.' "

There exists hardly a nation on earth that England has not politically and morally chained to slavery by reason of her unbridled egoism and covetousness. The German Empire alone avoided this fate. There are France and Russia, who, because of the regicide at Sarajevo, were made her tools and accomplices in order to carry out the English purposes. And should they be unable to accomplish this, then England herself will also jump in. Subterfuges, in order to attack Germany, can readily be invented by England and the world. Worthy reasons can easily be found. Two hundred years ago they gave the candid reason, "to destroy Dutch trade," but such a reason will not, above all things, be given by any Englishman at this time. At that time, when they were seeking grounds for war, the English Admiral spoke up: "Why hunt for reasons? What we need is a larger share of the trade which is now possessed by the Dutch. That is sufficient reason."

And now the same thing is applied to Germany. As far back as 1897, the English periodical, *Saturday Review,* spoke the truth clearly enough when it said, "England's prosperity can only be assured by the conquest of Germany. In case Germany were exterminated to-morrow, there would, the following morning, be not a single Englishman on earth who would not be so much the richer. Nations have fought for years over a state or a matter of succession (to a throne)—must they not now carry on a war over the yearly trade of so and so many milliards?"

Yes, she will go to war at the proper time, the time most propitious to her. Whether the time be now or later, whether it be by immediately jumping into the armed conflict, or not until the end of the war when Germany has been weakened, but she will surely come. It is her war, which she has been stirring up for many years. The last free country must now be given proofs of England's unbridled egoism and covetousness.

"Battery ready," "torpedo-tubes ready," "engines and auxiliaries ready," "repair party ready," "steering-gear ready," "signal and radio apparatus ready."

These reports were made one after the other in such rapid succession that I was torn from my thoughts. A hasty inspection of the ship and then I could report to the captain, "The ship is cleared for action."

At 15 knots we steamed toward Tsushima Straits. War watches were set on the *Emden* as darkness approached. This was done as follows: One-half the crew stood watch at their stations for action at the guns, searchlights, lookout, torpedo-room and in the engine- and fire-rooms, while the other half were permitted to sleep in their clothes ready to hasten to their stations in case of necessity. The captain took charge of one watch, the 1st officer of the other watch.

The *Emden* was heading northward toward Tsushima

Straits. The night was pitch dark, no moonlight. Nothing could be seen in the distance. Of course the ship was darkened. All lights visible from outboard were covered and torching at the smokepipes avoided.

Much phosphorescence, caused by the moderate speed, lighted up the sea. The swirling water, caused by the propellers, showed up as light-green streaks which could be seen far astern of the ship. The high waves climbing over the bow and breaking over the ship's sides amidships, throwing spray in all directions, covered the ship so that she looked as if she had been dipped into a red-green gold. Various large surfaces of elongated forms were sighted in the water so that the lookouts repeatedly reported submarines in sight. At 4 A.M. the port watch, which I commanded, was relieved. The captain took charge. Day began to break. I had hardly reached my room and prepared to get some sleep when I was awakened by the shrill calls of the alarm bells and the loud stamping of many running feet. "Clear ship for action," was passed from one compartment to another. And now everybody was ready at his battle station. Were we really lucky enough to meet a Russian or a Frenchman on the first day, as our dispatches indicated them to be in the neighborhood of Vladivostok?

The vibration of the ship indicated that meantime the engines were working up to high speed. In the gray daylight we saw, dead ahead, a large vessel, lights out, that appeared to be a man-of-war. The captain was approaching her at full speed. The ship had hardly seen us when she came about in short order and headed away from us. Heavy black clouds issued from her smokepipes, a sign that her engines were working at full power. The pursued vessel immediately set a course for the Japanese Islands, about 15 sea-miles away. A heavy smoke cloud hung close to the water and soon enveloped us entirely. As we could see only the mast heads, we had no means as yet of recognizing the ship. But her actions clearly showed that she was not a neutral vessel. Of this, however, more later.

Meantime it became light. The signal, "Stop at once," flew from our foremast. As the order did not, after a certain time, produce results, it was followed by a blank shot, and, as even this did no good, we fired a few shells at her. There was now no more use of the steamer's trying to reach neutral Japanese waters. When our shell fell close aboard her, she stopped, turned around and hoisted the Russian flag at all mast heads. And so, in the first night of the war, we took our first prize. It was foreseen, on the whole, that this would be the first German prize. She was the Russian volunteer steamer *Rjesan*. During peace she plied the passenger trade between Shanghai and Vladivostok. During war she would be armed and used as an auxiliary cruiser. She was a brand new, speedy ship, built at the German works of Schichau.

The *Emden* and her prize rolled considerably in the heavy sea. It was not a simple matter to lower the cutter which was to carry the prize crew from the *Emden* to the *Rjesan*. The boat was in great danger of smashing against the ship's side. But everything went well. Soon we saw our prize officer, followed by several men armed with pistols, climbing the gangway. The Russian flag was hauled down. In its place the German flag was hoisted. As the steamer could be of use in many ways—it could have been converted into a beautiful auxiliary cruiser—the captain gave up the idea of destroying her and decided to take her to Tsingtao. At 15 knots we proceeded to the southward. Behind us, in column, followed the *Rjesan*. On her was a prize crew, consisting of one officer and 12 men, in order to supervise the handling of the ship, machinery, etc., according to our orders.

The Russian captain made two strong protests against our taking her. She was a peaceful merchantman and it was therefore unjust to divert her. Above all he did not understand this. His knowledge of the rights of the sea was pretty weak. Our question as to why he had attempted to run away from us he allowed to remain unanswered. The captain had him informed that his fate would be decided in Tsingtao.

The *Emden* did not take the shortest way there. Hardly had the captain of the prize noted this than he again protested, desiring to be brought to port by the shortest route. His reason, naturally, was that he feared we might encounter other Russian ships on the course we were now steering. And that was exactly our intention. We had no news as to which courses the Russian vessels were taking, but, from the strenuous protests of the captain, we concluded that we might have an opportunity of capturing one or two more. Unfortunately no more were sighted. Of course his protest was not heeded, but instead our captain had him informed that the proceedings of the *Emden* were none of his business and further advised him of the results that might follow his continued obstinacy. After that we heard no more from our Russian neighbor. He must have felt confident that our promise to him would be carried out.

According to newspaper reports we discovered that the French fleet, consisting of the armored cruisers *Montcalm, Dupleix,* and several torpedo-boat destroyers, should be cruising about Vladivostok. We dared not meet these in daylight. As we rounded the southern extremity of Korea the lookout in the top reported—"Seven smoke clouds to starboard." In order to be absolutely sure, the captain sent me to the top. I also saw seven distinct smoke clouds and the upper part of the superstructure of a small vessel that appeared closest to ours just over the horizon. When I reported this the captain gave the order to turn away. We made a big sweep and cruised completely around the enemy. We arrived at Tsingtao without having been annoyed.

En route we picked up a very interesting radio message. The esteemed Reuter Bureau, known all over the world for its love of the truth, sent a message which informed the shuddering readers, "*Emden* has been sunk." We also shuddered to the marrow.

During the coming night our prize caused us a little more trouble. Naturally she also had to darken ship. But that was easier to order than to accomplish. On board the steamer were numerous married women passengers who were in great fear of what the barbarous hordes of Germans might do to them. Most of them were fat Russian Jewesses. Every few minutes one of them would turn on the lights in her cabin, so that finally the prize officer had to break the electric circuit at the dynamo. Thereupon they began to wander about with open lights which naturally could also not be permitted. On arrival at Tsingtao, the *Rjesan* was overhauled. The ship was still brand new, so that the Russians had not, as yet, had sufficient opportunity to ruin the good German machinery. Our prize could still do better than 17 knots. Therefore she was equipped with guns, manned by a German crew and set out as an auxiliary cruiser under the name of *Cormoran*.[1]

Tsingtao was given over to war preparations, the mine fields had been planted, the land fortifications along the coast were manned, and feverish work was going on in the harbor. A great number of German steamers lay inside the mole. Some of these were also being fitted out as auxiliary cruisers, some were being filled with coal in order to act as tenders to the squadron. Our captain received orders here from our squadron commander, Count von Spee. This squadron, consisting of the armored cruisers *Scharnhorst* and *Gneisnau* and the small cruiser *Nürnberg,* was in the South Sea steaming northward. The *Emden* was directed to intercept the squadron at a pre-determined rendezvous in the South Sea.

1. TRANSLATOR'S NOTE.—The old German gunboat *Cormorant* was being dismantled at Tsingtao. Her captain and most of her crew were transferred to the newly converted auxiliary cruiser *Cormoran* (ex-*Rjesan*), which sailed from Tsingtao and eventually interned at Guam.

CHAPTER 2

To the Southward

THAT DAY AND ALL THROUGH the night all hands aboard worked feverishly. We had to coal, taking on as much as we could possibly hold, receive a great quantity of all sorts of material, increase our personnel, and make all the many preparations for war. At sunrise the next day the *Emden* left Tsingtao, followed by a great number of German ships that were going forth to meet the squadron. In the harbor there was much enthusiasm. Everybody on land envied us. As long as the war existed only with France and Russia, Tsingtao would hardly be concerned. Likewise it was unnecessary to worry about the state of the land fortifications. On the sea side were good and sufficient works that could not be destroyed by ships. The land forts, inasmuch as only a few had been constructed, were merely small and unpretentious earthworks, solely for infantry usages. Still, an attack on the land side was not to be feared as Tsingtao was entirely surrounded by the neutral territory of China.

Calm, clear weather prevailed as the *Emden* slowly steamed out of the inner harbor. Our band played "The Watch on the Rhein." The entire crew was on deck and joined in singing.

Cheers were given on all sides. All were highly confident. Here was reproduced, on a smaller scale, the same war-enthusiasm as was being shown in Germany.

The *Emden* proceeded cautiously through the openings in the mine fields. The sun had just risen. There lay Tsingtao, the crown of the Far East, golden red in the light of the first sun rays of the young day. A picture of peace. Along the beach were long rows of clean, artistically constructed houses. The whole overlooked by the Signal Mountain. In the background were the brown stone mountains covered with a new dress of fresh, young and green forests. The church tower and its cross stood forth prominently in the light, reddish vapors of the morning haze. Further to the right the pretty and clean bar-racks, the government house, the bathing beach. The whole picture circled with white, the surf arising from the heaving bosom of the sea and breaking on the cliffs along the coast. Glittering pearls and diamonds were strewn in full measure by Neptune on this precious gown of nature. The charms of the farm and German industry have here produced a picture of fairyland where previously had been such a useless and rough region. All of us were in very sentimental moods. But the service called with an iron "must." Therefore tear yourself from this picture! On to the south!

The steamer *Markomannia* followed us, the other steamers steering different courses. *Markomannia* remained a faithful follower to us for several months.

On the way to the South Sea we received the radio telling us of the rupture of diplomatic relations between Germany and England and of the declaration of war by England. We were not surprised at this, and if we were a little astounded, it was due to the fact that the wire-puller of all evil had, for the first time in a hundred years, brought her own bones into danger. A few days later we were notified of the ridiculous ultimatum of Japan; which did not disturb us very much. A clean-up, that was the intention of them all.

On leaving Tsingtao, war with England and Japan had not

yet been declared. Later on we read in the English papers that our escape from Tsingtao was only due to the fact that in passing a Japanese armored cruiser on blockade we hoisted the English flag and gave three cheers to our allied brothers.

Does this report originate perhaps in the suggestion that the English and Japanese men-of-war were already on their way to Tsingtao before war was declared?

In any event the whole report was perfectly ridiculous. Entirely apart from the subject, that we ever disgraced our good ship by the hoisting of the English rag, we most certainly would not have missed the chance, when passing the Japanese, of sending him a torpedo greeting.

It is strange how systematic lying will harmonize with logic.

During the evening of August 12, we came in the neighborhood of the island where we expected to meet the cruiser squadron and found the outpost vessels. In the middle lay the powerful cruisers *Scharnhorst* and *Gneisenau*, with colliers alongside busy coaling. Farther to the left the slender *Nürnberg*, also engaged in coaling. Scattered about in the harbor were a number of large and small tenders and auxiliaries of the squadron. The *Emden* was ordered to anchor in the right half of the harbor, close to the flagship. Rousing cheers were exchanged between ships as we passed the other vessels and soon thereafter our anchor splashed—the last time for a long while.

The captain reported aboard the flagship for orders from the squadron commander, and made the proposal to him to detach the *Emden* from the squadron and to send her to the Indian Ocean to carry on a cruise of "commerce destruction."

The next day saw the squadron in column, followed by the colliers, on an easterly course. The squadron commander had not yet made known his decision in regard to our captain's proposal and we were all eager to know what his conclusions were. Along toward midday several signals were hoisted high on the flagship: "*Emden* detached, wish you much success," read the signal. In an elegant turn our ship sheered out of column, a "thank-you" signal for the squadron commander's wishes at the mast head, then a semaphore to the *Markomannia*, "Remain with *Emden*," and soon, on an opposite course, we lost sight of the other ships of the squadron. All knew that we had seen each other for the last time.

It was a long trip to our particular scene of operations. It was tormenting not to have advices as to whether war existed with Japan or not. The German radio station at Yap had already been destroyed by the English. After cruising for a week we fell in with the German steamer *Princess Alice*. We took several reservists aboard and then sent her toward Manila. On the high seas we later on met our small gun-boat *Geier*. For lack of signal communication she did not have exact information of the war, nor any of that which concerned England and Japan. We remained together but a short time, exchanged such information as we had and the *Geier* then cruised to the eastward to follow the squadron. Our voyage again proceeded in the direction of our future hunting ground.

The days were right strenuous for the crew as we had to maintain war watches in order to be prepared for all emergencies. There was no opportunity to give the crew any recreation. We had no harbor in which we would be safe. A Japanese steamer, that we met en route, had to be left alone, unfortunately, as the ultimatum period had not expired, and as we had no information as yet as to whether war had been declared.

Evidently thinking that he was dealing with one of his boon companions, the yellow one made a most profound salute with his flag when passing us. The greeting remained unanswered.

We had now reached the point where, in order to reach the open ocean, we had to pass through the narrow straits. These straits swarmed with fishing craft and such other small ships. The nights being bright moonlight, the *Emden* was visible for a considerable distance. The captain did not relish the idea of meeting so many sailing vessels. He spoke to me about it, saying that he wished to avoid meeting any sort of ship for fear our presence and course in those waters would become known to everybody. All the English men-of-war had either two or four smokepipes; none had three like the *Emden*. Then I conceived the idea of building us a fourth smokepipe. Immediately I had all the deckstrips brought out. These are rolls of heavy sail cloth, about two meters wide, laid on the decks as a protection to the linoleum. In the upper end we sewed a wooden batten and then hoisted this improvised smokepipe forward of our regular forward smokepipe. As viewed from the side the effect was good. But from forward its appearance was exceedingly faulty; it did not have the necessary thickness of its step-brothers. It was only a few millimeters thick. But in the hurry of that first night, nothing better could be accomplished. I proposed to the captain to build a better fourth smokepipe, to which he agreed. And the next day we began the work. Soon we had built, by means of wooden laths and sail cloth, an elegant smokepipe, and when this was in place we resembled the English cruiser *Yarmouth*. I purposely had the smokepipe made oval as the *Yarmouth* had one that shape. Our trailer *Markomannia* was ordered out to a position on our beam, and according to her suggestions (by signal) we improved the position of the fourth smokepipe. We then painted the marks to simulate overheating of the outer casting of the smokepipe, so that from now on we could, at any time, day or night, hoist our fake.

And so we arrived in the Bay of Bengal at the end of the first week in September. For about five days an English warship, probably the *Minotaur*, steamed parallel to and close by us, as we knew by the strength of her radio signals. By and by her signals became weaker until they ceased entirely. We did not sight her.

CHAPTER 3

On the Hunt

FINALLY, DURING THE NIGHT OF September 10, our work began. A steamer came in sight and we approached her to have a closer look. Ship darkened, silently we stole up on our prey from aft. The captain approached to within a hundred meters of the steamer who, after the fashion of merchantmen, was peacefully going ahead and bothering about nothing except what might be sighted ahead with lights showing. Through the quiet, calm night the megaphone broke forth with "Stop immediately! Do not use your radio! We are sending a boat aboard!" The steamer did not seem to thoroughly comprehend this. Perhaps she did not expect an enemy ship to appear here in the heart of the Indian Ocean, or did she possibly imagine it to be the voices of the sea gods that accosted her? In any event, she kept peacefully on. As a calling card we sent her a blank shot. Then she realized what was happening, went astern four bells and a jingle—we felt sorry for the poor machinists whom she so rudely awakened, blew her siren, and yelled her willingness to obey our orders. Our cutter with the prize crew took the water and went over to take possession of the steamer. Then we suddenly received somewhat of a shock: "This is the Greek steamer *Pontoporros*," was the signal we received from the ship. That certainly was unfortunate. The first steamer had to be a neutral one. Then most certainly would the entire coast soon know that a German man-of-war was in the Indian Ocean. The richest prizes would therefore escape us. God be praised, however, because the precious Greek had contraband on board, namely, coal destined to English harbors. She was, therefore, the *Markomannia* being now half empty, welcomed as a most thankful contribution to our squadron, which now consisted of three ships. These would not be the only ones.

The *Pontoporros* had a cargo of Indian coal on board, the dirtiest coal that can be imagined. I had hoped to replenish our diminished stock of stores from the prizes. For six weeks the *Emden* had not been in port and could therefore obtain no supplies. The 1st Officer is the housewife of the ship and is responsible for every small detail in regard to the obtaining of supplies and equipment. Before leaving Tsingtao I had packed the ship as full as possible with everything that could be necessary or desirable. In the last few days, however, it became evident that we were rapidly approaching the end of our stock of soap. The portions that were issued to the men at first were now becoming much smaller. About 14 days more and we would reach the point where washing could be classed as a luxury. Therefore, I had jokingly told the captain to pick out a soap-boat for me as his first prize. Instead I drew a ship load of Indian coal. I could not refrain from tearing up to the captain, blood in my eye, to protest, but he laughingly promised to do his level best to keep on the hunt to provide me with soap. And he kept his word. Very early in the morning of September 11, a few hours after our squadron had received its first addition, with the rising of the sun, a large steamer appeared dead ahead who, thinking we were an English man-of-war, was so overjoyed at our presence that she hoisted a huge British flag while still at a great distance. I do not know what kind of expression came over her captain's face when we hoisted our flag and invited him most graciously to tarry with us awhile. The steamer had left Calcutta and, having been detailed for transport duty between Colombo and France, was fitted out in fine style. Especially were we touched by the fact that she did not disown the English desire for cleanliness and therefore had taken such a big cargo of soap that our small crew, itself in the greatest need of this most necessary assistant to Kultur, would have enough to last a whole year. We also found a beautiful race horse aboard. A bullet behind the ear saved the animal the agonies of a death by drowning. We had less compassion for the numerous built-in, beautifully numbered, horse stalls and gun mounts aboard the ship. A half hour later the sharks could, at closer quarters, occupy their attention with these.

The crew of the ship was transported to our "lucky bag." The "lucky bag" was always one of the captured ships which was either empty or in ballast and therefore of little value, or which contained neutral cargo and could therefore not be sunk without a loss. At the end of the war, all neutral cargo destroyed must be paid for. The "lucky bag" always followed along behind the *Emden* until she was finally filled up with people taken from the captured vessels. Then she was detached and sent into the nearest harbor. Under these circumstances, the *Pontoporros* was detailed to the role of "lucky bag."

In the next few days our business expanded. It happened somewhat as follows:

When a steamer came up, it was stopped and an officer with about 10 men sent aboard. They prepared the ship for sinking and gave the necessary orders for the disembarkation of the passengers, etc. While we were so occupied, the next mast head would, according to rule, appear over the horizon. We had no need of hurrying. The steamers came willingly right up to us. When the next ship approached to the proper distance, the *Emden* steamed ahead to meet her, made a friendly signal, which notified her to proceed close aboard our previously captured steamer. Then again an officer and some men would go aboard, prepare that steamer for sinking, give the necessary orders for disembarking the passengers, etc., and when this was concluded, the third mast head would bob up. The *Emden* approached her and the same process would be repeated. In this way we have had five or six steamers together at one spot. Of these, one would still show the tops of her smokepipes, the next would be sunk to the level of her decks, the third would be almost normal, but showing, by reason of her swaying back and forth, that she was beginning to go down. The passengers of our captured steamers would then make the most astonishing acquaintances aboard our "lucky bag."

So we grazed around in the region between Ceylon and Calcutta. With us were traveling our old follower the *Markomannia* and the Greek collier *Pontoporros*, which had meantime transferred her duties as "lucky bag" to the steamer *Cabinga*. This was an English steamer with an American cargo, that was not sunk because of the cost of the cargo.

The *Cabinga* accompanied us for several days. She, the *Markomannia*, and the *Pontoporros* were not the only *Emden* followers this night. During our journey we made some more prizes, but these, in the interest of the passengers, were not to be sunk until daylight, because of the seaway and the darkness. All told we had six followers that night. Of these, three disappeared under the surface of the sea the next morning. The *Cabinga* herself, with the passengers, was sent away. The captain's wife and small child were also aboard the *Cabinga*. The spot where the other steamers were sunk was so far from land that it was impossible for a boat to safely reach the coast. In anticipation of having his ship sunk, the captain of the *Cabinga* begged us to allow him, in case he be set adrift in a boat, to carry along a pistol with which to protect his wife and child. This was a typical example of the wrong impressions which the deceitful English press spreads among its countrymen. We would simply be following the tales of the English press if we, hundreds of miles from the coast, were to place women and children in open boats and allow them to starve.

When we told the captain that his ship would not be sunk he was beside himself with joy. I myself visited him aboard his ship for several hours. He could not properly express himself, begged me to carry his thanks to our captain, and also gave me a letter with the request that I present it to the captain on my return. In this letter he again thanked us for the humane treatment which he and his family had received. The prize officer and crew who were aboard his ship had conducted themselves as gentlemen. He could not find sufficient words of praise for the behavior of the Germans. The captain himself would never forget the way he had been treated. He was received by his adversaries in much the same friendly and honorable way in which one seaman treats another seaman when in need in times of peace. He would do all he could to spread the truth in the English newspapers.

I had a long conversation with his wife. She said about the same things to me that her husband wrote in the letter. During the conversation she discovered that my oilskins were pretty badly in need of repair and she begged me most earnestly to take along the oilskins of her husband. Further, she entreated us, as we were hard up for smoking tobacco, to take as much tobacco and as many cigarettes as we could carry along with us. These were mere trifles with which they could show their appreciation.

Naturally, we left without taking oilskins or tobacco.

On leaving, the *Cabinga*'s decks were loaded with people, all passengers of the captured steamers. And on our calling out to them, "You may proceed," the answer consisted in three cheers for the captain, the officers, and the crew of H.M.S. *Emden*, "Hurra! Hurra! Hurra!" All the people on the decks of the *Cabinga* joined in the cheering. How many there were can be best explained by quoting an English paper, which later on fell into our hands, in which was described the *Cabinga* on entering Calcutta as appearing not like a merchantman, but, from the number of persons to be found aboard, one could easily have imagined her to have been something like a school-ship. There were at least 400 people on board her.

Also, later on in our wanderings, whenever our "lucky bags," full of passengers from sunken ships, were detached, we always received our three hurras. It seems to be an English custom to reward the murdering of small children and the killing of women and men by giving three cheers.

I wish to insert here a few remarks concerning the actions of the English when their steamers were captured. Most of them were very sensible. As soon as they had recovered from their first surprise, they would indulge in a series of complaints concerning their government, but, with one exception, never opposed the sinking of the ship. We always gave them plenty of time to gather up their private possessions. They usually devoted this time trying to save their valuable cargo of whiskey before the fishes could get at it. I can honestly say that we seldom delivered a crowd of sober Englishmen to the "lucky bag." After all, however, they never forgot their "business" and endeavored by every possible means to make the ships of the rival lines fall prey to the German privateering. Usually, when the captains left their ships, they would say: "Tell me, have you seen the steamer X?" We replied: "No!" "What," returned the captain, "haven't you seen her? Why she was steaming only two hours behind and seven miles south of me!"

By this means we always knew in advance the name of the next ship as soon as her mast heads appeared, and in this way avoided the embarrassment of meeting neutrals.

Especially pleased was one captain who found himself in the disagreeable position of having to pilot a dredger from England to Australia. Every seaman will sympathize with this poor devil for having to deliver to Australia such a wallowing tub, which could not make more than four knots. And so the captain was very much pleased at being captured by us, a fact easily understood by any unbiased person. Seldom have I witnessed such exulting pleasure in any man. It certainly was quite a trick to bring the rolling and pitching dredger this far. And tears of gratitude ran down his rough seaman's cheeks as he cried, "Thank God, I am rid of that tub! I certainly have long since earned that £500 which I was to receive for taking her to Australia."

A seaman always has a peculiar feeling when he sees a ship sinking. Even we, accustomed to helping vessels in distress, were affected not a little by the sight of sinking vessels, even those that we had to destroy. The destruction was usually done in the following way:

We went into the engine-room and removed the bonnet of a main overboard discharge valve. The water immediately came into the engine-room in a stream twice a man's height and more than a man's thickness. The watertight doors to the adjoining fire-room were opened and secured against closing, so that at least two large compartments of the ship would certainly fill up with water. In addition, two smaller compartments were also filled, either by exploding bombs—this at night—or by firing shells into them. For a time the ship would totter about as if she did not know what to do with herself. Deeper and deeper she would sink until finally the rail would be awash. The waves would eagerly lap over the decks of the doomed vessel. It seemed as if unseen hands were pulling and tearing at her in order to seize their prey as soon as possible. A shudder seemed to run through her whole structure. This was possibly a shiver of fear of the ship's body, as if she were making a final heroic attempt to avoid her fate. Then came the surrender, the collapse. The bow sank, the masts came up flat on the water, the rudder and screws rose, the stern high in the air. The smokepipe blew out the last cloud of steam and soot. For a few seconds the vessel would remain standing vertically, and then, like a stone, shoot down into the depths. The air pressure would blow up the last few compartments or spaces in the stern. Columns of water, meters high, would be forced by the air pressure out of all openings, ventilators, and port holes. Then a swirling whirl, the sea closed over her, and nothing more remained to be seen of the ship. As a last greeting from the deep, about a half minute later, the loose spars, beams, boats, and such truck would come to the surface. The long planks of wood would shoot up vertically, like arrows, jumping several meters clear out of the water. The final marks of recognition of the spot where the ship sank consisted in a large oil slick, a few broken up boats, beams, life buoys, and such. Then the *Emden* would go ahead to meet the next oncoming mast head.

The English were extremely grateful for our allowing them sufficient time to save all their personal belongings. They also reported this in their newspapers. I am not stretching the point when I say that at the end of 1914, the *Emden* was the best-beloved ship in the East Indies. As a whole, the English had no understanding of this war. To them it is not a national war as it is with us; instead, they stand off indifferently and laud the achievements of friend and foe alike, solely from a sportive interest viewpoint. And so it happened that it was possible for the Indian newspapers to honor our captain and his ship in song and story. The captain was called "The Gentleman Captain," and the papers said "He played the game and was playing it well."

We treated those passengers well who behaved properly— which they nearly all did—and always met them at least halfway, and we did not hesitate to sacrifice ourselves in order to make them comfortable. That reminds me of a case when, shortly before sinking a ship, an Englishman came to me and asked that he might retain his sole treasure, that which was dearest to his heart, namely, his motorcycle. The motorcycle was taken out of the cargo space—a job that is not very easy— and was sent along with its owner, who was so touched that he could hardly speak, in a special steamer to our "lucky bag," where they both evidently felt happier.

Another Englishman had quite the contrary experience. He

was a very superior sort of gentleman. He was "traffic master" of Calcutta, and was taking passage on a vessel bound for Colombo where he was to transfer the ship to the transport service. His plans were shot to pieces. This made him very peevish. In hunting for "trade" many otherwise approachable Englishmen become exceedingly sensitive. While the ship was being prepared for sinking, he packed his numerous patent-leather trunks and piled them up on deck. Then, with the superior air of one of the sons of the "Albion Rulers of the Sea," with his pipe in the corner of his mouth, his hands in the pockets of his large-checked trousers, he went up on the bridge and promenaded back and forth. His contemptuous glances were cast at the "Germans." He bothered no more about his trunks. He assumed that, at the proper time, we would come to him for orders in regard to the disposition of the trunks. Finally all the other people with their impedimenta had left the ship. The ship was ready to be sunk. In single solitary grandeur the "traffic master," checked trousers, pipe stump and all, still promenaded the bridge. He was told that it was now time for him to leave. His answer was merely a mute indication with the thumb of his right hand, which he removed from his trousers pockets for this special occasion, toward his pile of trunks that, by its glittering isolation, still graced the deck of the ship. Evidently he concluded that his regal attitude was sufficient to make us especially attentive toward the looking-after of those trunks of his—"The Traffic Master of Calcutta." Our men no doubt misunderstood him. They quietly concluded that he did not care what became of his trunks. These, after this experience, went overboard all alone. The same would have happened to him had he not speedily left the ship. The last boat was about to leave. The "traffic master" then descended, first from the heights of his English dignity, then from the heights of the bridge, quickly grabbed up the smallest box that remained and hurriedly carried it off the ship. Our men accompanied him, hands in their trousers pockets, cigarettes in the corners of their mouths.

All of our original supplies had naturally long since become exhausted. But, thanks to the thoughtfulness of the English, the captured steamers were so well supplied with conserved provisions by the best English firms that our men had to exercise the greatest self-restraint in order to carry out our mission—*i.e.*, enemy goods must under all circumstances be destroyed. Especially did we prove that candy and confectionery and such other tasty bits, because of their cognac contents, were not unsuitable even to sailormen's palates.

In the neighborhood of Calcutta we made the little-to-be-desired acquaintance of a steamer by the name of *Loredano*. Though she failed to hoist a flag, she could readily be identified as an Italian from a distance, because she was literally incrusted with filth of all sorts. Not finding anything suspicious when examining her, we had to permit this neutral vessel to proceed. This happened just at a time when we had gathered in another batch of ships and were commencing to send them on their downward journey. After sinking the last ship, and as the *Emden* was leaving the spot, we could still see the Italian busily engaged in fishing up the floating bales of tea that came from a large tea ship we had just sunk. Did he perhaps think these bales contained macaroni? We did not begrudge him this pleasure. But we were less pleased the next day to find out that this "neutral steamer" had made herself guilty of interfering with the rights of a commerce destroyer during war, by sending a radio notifying the entire region that the *Emden* was at hand.

As we had grazed about sufficiently in this region of the Bay of Bengal, and as we noticed that no more ships were arriving, we decided to shift our scene of operations, which was becoming more alluring each day, to the other side of the Bay, near Rangoon. And here we received our first serious setback in that not a single ship was running. Later on we read in the newspapers that the entire shipping was held up because of our presence. For all that we had to consider it a moral success that a Norwegian steamer had taken over the duties as "lucky bag" and that we were now free of our last troublesome guests. During our trip to Rangoon, we were not sighted for more than a week. This fact caused the circumspect English Indian Government, in the interests of its subjects and to officially announce the celebration to their patient countrymen, to spread the report that the *Emden* pest had now been successfully exterminated by her 16 pursuers, and that now the ocean trade could again be safely carried on. Of course we did not know this until later when we read of it in the newspapers. As merchantmen no longer appeared in our locality, we returned to the region of our former operations on the east coast of India. The captain decided to test the resistance of the oil tanks at Madras. The *Emden* appeared off the harbor on the evening of September 18. There, the very day before, had the official announcement of the *Emden*'s loss been made. In order to properly celebrate, a hilarious crowd had assembled that night in the club. As we did not know this at that time, we unfortunately were not responsible that our shells dropped into the soup of the diners. Otherwise we would naturally have postponed our bombardment for one day. One should never unnecessarily irritate one's foe. Holy institutions must be treated with as much clemency as possible. And especially in regard to his "dinner" is the Englishman sensitive.

We approached to within about 3000 meters of Madras. The lighthouse threw its friendly beams out over the harbor. It made our navigation quite simple, for which we gave our unanimous thanks to the high government of this place. In the searchlight beam we saw our object, the high, white, red-topped oil tanks. A few shells thrown into them, several pillars of bluish-yellow jets of flame, a red, burning stream running out of one of the shot holes, an immense, heavy, black cloud, and, in accordance with the old proverb, "A change makes for contentment," we had this time sent several millions into the air instead of into the sea.

On leaving Madras we were fired on without knowing from

what direction the shells came. But there were only a few shots fired and these evidently without aiming. Later on the English wrote in their newspapers that, when we were fired on, we doused our lights and quickly disappeared. To this I would remark that we of course first approached without any lights showing, and that both the captain and I did not notice that we were being fired on, of which we were later informed by our officers stationed aft. Therefore, we had no idea of withdrawing because of the firing. In regard to the lights, we did exactly the opposite. When we finished firing we lighted up the ship, that is, we purposely displayed many lights on our port side and headed north. Soon thereafter we again put out all lights and headed toward the south.

The fire at Madras lighted our way for a long time. The heavy, black smoke cloud of the burning oil was still visible the next day, even though we were over 90 sea-miles, that is, about 180 kilometers, away from Madras. By way of Pondicherry we kept on around Ceylon in order to honor the west coast of India with our presence.

As we later read in the newspapers, our bombardment of Madras resulted in the flight of all Europeans from the coast to the inland regions. In addition, the English established "searchlight service," that is, they played searchlights every night along the entire coast adjacent to their harbors. In this way they simplified our navigation very much, for which we again give our unanimous thanks to the far-sighted Indian Government of this section. On the evening of September 26, we were close to the harbor of Colombo. While cruising back and forth we suddenly saw a dark shadow in the searchlight beams which interested us very much. At a distance she seemed rather dangerous, but this danger lessened on her closer approach. It was an English steamer loaded to the eyes with sugar. The captain of this ship, which we captured under the very guns of the English forts, because he was sighted in the beams of the searchlights of his own war harbor, was so peeved that he objected to our orders. The deplorable result of this patriotic step on his part was that he was not allowed to take even a handkerchief along with him when he left his ship.

Within five minutes his ship was cleared and the crew transported to our "lucky bag." The captain and his engineer divided the honors of being permitted to inhabit one of the temporary cells aboard H.M.S. *Emden*. Ten minutes later the sugar steamer sweetened the suppers of the sharks.

This English captain, as we later found out in the newspapers, told some wonderful fairy tales about the *Emden*. He set forth that he was well treated, but when brought aboard the *Emden* he did not receive treatment according to his rank. Evidently he had an idea that our captain should vacate his cabin for him. Further, he spoke rather disapprovingly of the cleanliness of the *Emden*. She was said to be dirty, scarred, and dented, in which I cannot disagree with him. It is impossible to coal for weeks at a time in the open sea, or to carry a heavy, loose deck-load of coal, without being scarred. Had I had any idea that I would receive such a pleasant visit, I should have staked my reputation as a 1st Officer on my being able to show my guest a cleanly scrubbed and freshly painted ship.

In addition, this precious man said that our crew looked starved out and in low spirits. If our men appeared to be starved out it would mean that we failed to use the provisions which we found on the captured English ships, letting them go to waste instead. And the low spirits of the crew can best be illustrated by the fact that they knew of no greater enjoyment than to perform the best dancing steps before our guests during the daily after-dinner concert to the tunes of "I was at Shöneberg, in the month of May," or "Carousing and Drinking." Later on, perhaps, when our unwilling guest left the *Emden* in order to travel home aboard our next "lucky bag," he probably did not fare so well. Our prize officer, who remained aboard the "lucky bag" until she was detached, told us that the ship's officers of the sugar steamer cursed their captain out roundly. He himself was said to have been sufficiently insured against losses, but they were not. And through his obstinacy they had lost all their own possessions. As the captain came aboard the "lucky bag," his officers met him at the gangway with shirt sleeves rolled up. Perhaps he often wished that he had remained aboard the *Emden*.

In the meantime the question of coal supply was getting troublesome. Our faithful *Markomannia* was empty. We still had with us the other prize, *Pontoporros*, which was filled with Indian coal. The Indian coal, however, makes very heavy smoke clouds and deposits a great amount of soot in the boilers, so that our followers were not very pleased with our smoking them up. The question of better coal was decided, however, by the English Admiralty in a very useful and anticipatory manner; for, the very next day they sent us a fine 7000-ton steamer, full of the best English-Welsh coal, bound for Hong-Kong, but diverted for uses other than their own. With this we were well supplied with the best coal and our cares for a further supply of that commodity were put off for some future day. The captain of our latest collier did not hesitate to accept duty in the German service, and whistling "Rule Britannia," he thenceforth conducted himself aboard ship in a fair and honorable manner, the operation of the collier of course being supervised by one of our officers and a prize crew.

Meantime it became clear to even the English Government that the *Emden* had not as yet been wholly destroyed. Therefore, they again gave more orders to stop all trade. There was nothing for us to gain by remaining in that neighborhood. The captain, therefore, decided that during this pause we would devote some attention to the *Emden*, which had been at sea for such a long time. It was especially necessary to scrape the long grass off the ship's bottom. And so we started south.

CHAPTER 4

The Flying Dutchman

W E KNEW THAT 16 ENEMY VESSELS, consisting of English, French, Russian, and Japanese were on our trail. Information in regard to their positions or their names was denied us. But it made little difference, as the *Emden* was the smallest and least powerful of the cruisers in the Eastern Asiatic. Any opponent whom we might meet would be more powerful. It was clear to everybody on board that the *Emden* could not continue her rôle much longer. Sufficient hounds will surely kill the rabbit. Even in case of meeting an enemy cruiser that was not much too powerful for us, we must still suffer such damage and such a large loss in personnel in the fight, that we would have to leave our scene of operations. There was not a single harbor where we could go for repairs. Above all, it would be impossible to replace the losses in personnel. The captain had taken this view at the beginning of our operations and therefore decided that it was the *Emden*'s duty to inflict as much damage as possible before she, sooner or later, came to grief.

We knew by means of the radio signals that our enemies were all around us, and often close by. Although we could not decipher the messages, which were in secret codes, still we could estimate by the strength of the signals how far away the sending ship was. However, we did not derive much advantage from this as our enemies were frequently on all sides of us. Instead of slipping by them we might possibly run right into them. The English have frequently said that the *Emden* eluded them so long because of her high speed. That is not correct. Even apart from the fact that her bottom had grown so foul as to make high speed impossible, the *Emden* still could not make more than 11 knots. The colliers, that were not any faster than that, had to be convoyed. Again, there was no need of higher speed. When going at 11 knots we might miss an enemy, while at 20 knots we might have walked right into the same enemy's arms. The radio messages received gave us a hint, luckily, as to which nation the ship belonged. The English sent differently than the French, and these differed from the Japanese, and these again sent differently than the Russians, because the last mentioned, when they could signal at all, did so very poorly.

The routine aboard was practically the same as during peace. Of course we had several more lookouts on watch at night. Naturally all guns and torpedoes were kept ready for action day and night.

The captain spent the greater part of his time on the bridge. There, in out-of-the-way corners, we placed comfortable chairs, so that he could sleep up there and still be constantly at hand, ready for a call whenever the occasion demanded it. During the day he busied himself looking over charts, sailing directions and such other sources of information. After hours of tedious work, he would draw up his plans, which the *Emden* was to follow so successfully. The devotion of the crew to the captain was touching. The men knew exactly what kind of leader they had and were proud of their ship which he so successfully commanded. Singing and other noises ceased very quickly when the word was passed, "The captain is tired." A single word of encouragement from the captain to the men, whether during a maneuver or when coaling ship, in spite of the heaviest work or the greatest exhaustion, brought the most astonishing results. Often enough, while going through the ship at night, have I heard the men sitting in the dark discussing the captain. "Yes, our captain, he knows how to do it." That was approximately the gist of their remarks.

Life in the officers' mess was also practically the same as in peace times. The mess rooms were not quite as comfortable. All woodwork was removed; curtains and other inflammable material were taken down. Transporting ammunition and such took place through the mess rooms day and night. The gun mounted in the ward room, had to be kept ready at all times. At night, all officers not on watch or at their battle stations, slept, during good weather, in hammocks on the poop, and during bad weather on mattresses and in hammocks in the mess rooms. Undressing was not customary. One had to be ready at all times.

The most pleasant hours were those spent reading the newspapers captured on the ships. That was our only connection with the whole outside world. Whenever it happened that we were mentioned in the English press, we could construct a fair estimate of the accuracy of their lying reports, especially if one had had previous experience with the Reuter Information Bureau. It was very comforting to us to follow our "disorderly retreat" out of France in the western campaign! Also we did not permit ourselves to be seriously disturbed over the enormous losses of German troops, even though when these were added together they considerably exceeded the total population of the entire German Empire.

Our own deeds were likewise reviewed in the English light through their Indian newspapers, and we were somewhat astounded to see how the English took it. They seemed to think the whole thing a huge joke, made comic remarks about their own numerous ships that could not catch us, joked about the shooting-up of the Madras oil reservoirs, nominated our captain as an honorary member of their best club in Calcutta, and published a long series of *Emden* stories. These were so untruthful that one need only set them forth as base counterfeits of a race as irresponsible as the English. A few of them are recounted.

In one of the Indian papers appeared an account of a merchant captain who said he had met the *Emden* without being captured. The mere fact, that this story was believed, definitely proves the gullibility of the English reading public. Because any English steamer captain that ever met the *Emden* never again left her with his ship. The captain went on to say, "I steered for Sand Head light-ship at night, but found it out of its accustomed position; but soon thereafter I saw the pilot boat which turned its searchlight on me. (For the reader's benefit, I will add that it is usually customary in that locality to equip pilot boats with searchlights in order to draw ships toward them.) I proceeded with my steamer toward the pilot ship, but was astonished to find that I was not getting any closer to her; instead of the pilot ship coming closer to me she was running away. I ordered my engineer to raise all steam possible and to work up to full power. In spite of this the distance remained the same. Over this unusual maneuver of the pilot, I cudgeled my brains. Before I had arrived at a conclusion my astonishment rose to hitherto unmeasured heights when I saw the pilot boat commence to make small and then ever increasingly large circles. I went astern in a wild attempt to cut off a chord of his circle and thereby get nearer to him. My signal with the steam whistle accomplished nothing. Neither was I able to reach the pilot boat. After I had gone astern like mad for about a half hour, the pilot boat extinguished her searchlight and left me in total ignorance. I later on learned that this pilot boat was the *Emden*."

So much for the tale of this captain. Ingenuous angel!

Another *Emden* yarn came out in the Calcutta paper in which was stated:

One day the government received an urgent radio message that said an English cruiser, coming from Singapore, had burned up all her coal in chasing the *Emden* and now was slowly heading toward an Indian port, burning chests, beds, furniture, etc. It was urgently requested that several thousand tons of coal be hurried to this port. The efficient and zealous government immediately took special steps to pass the order along to some subordinates to carry out. These subordinates, also wishing to do something for the good of their fatherland, passed the order along to some other subordinates. These again, filled to the brim with zealous energy, and also wishing to do something, finally decided to turn the now voluminous correspondence and orders over to a coal firm. These last, seeing an opportunity to make some money, finally actually set to work. Hundreds and hundreds of coolies were employed, mountains of coal were quickly loaded into the trains, day and night the work continued feverishly and uninterruptedly. Shortly thereafter, train after train, filled with steeple-high loads of black diamonds, began to roll into the harbor at the hitherto unheard-of speed of 40 kilometers per hour. In the meantime extensive preparations were going on in the harbor in order to expedite the coaling of the English warship. No precious time must be lost in capturing the *Emden*.

Most astonished—which was rather pleasing in the case of the coolies, but less pleasant in the case of the others concerned—were the railroad officials, the captain of the port, and the inhabitants of the city, and especially displeasing in the case of the wounded feelings of the coal firm and the government, when finally no English cruiser appeared. Eventually some light was thrown on this dark affair. After much thinking the Indian Government finally found the solution. "*The Radio was sent by the Emden.*" The government did not tell its readers how the *Emden* could possibly have sent this message in cipher without having a copy of their secret code.

In this way many so-called "*Emden* stories" were published. On board we composed a theatrical skit on all these yarns, but unfortunately it was lost later on.

The crew had a great deal of spare time. It was impracticable to carry on drills as in times of peace. A considerable portion of the crew was always busy either on watch on deck or in the engineer's department. The remainder had to be constantly kept in first class physical condition to provide against any possible unknown contingencies of war. During good weather the majority of the crew slept on their battle stations at the guns. The engineer's personnel especially had to be provided with good airy places to sleep. The extraordinary intense heat made it impossible for them to sleep in their allotted quarters. Therefore, we set aside for them a certain place on deck and made preparations for swinging their hammocks there. So it happened that during fair weather at night on deck a regular "sleeping army" swung lightly back and forth in their hammocks.

Frequently we issued reports of the war or as much as we might know of them. The newspapers were read to them and the private books of the officers were loaned to the men up forward to give them some diversion.

The duty of publishing the war bulletins to the men I reserved for myself. We made a large chart of Germany and the surrounding countries, and on this we traced the lines of land conquest.

It was not an easy matter for me to come to a conclusion as to the best way in which to impart the war news to the men. We were entirely dependent on English newspapers which printed, as I knew, the most unreasonable and distorted reports. Constant defeat of armies, perfect disintegration all around, complete collapse, famines, revolutions, suicide epidemics among army leaders, were the order of the day. The Crown Prince was killed, the Kaiser had been wounded, Bavaria had seceded from the Empire, and such idiotic nonsense.

I might have made up a résumé of the newspaper reports and published this to the crew, omitting the crudest of the English falsehoods. It was very possible that the morale of the men would suffer if they continued to hear these constantly depressing reports from home. On the other hand, I had to admit to myself that the contents of the papers could not forever remain unknown to the crew. My mess-boy would probably see and read the newspapers in my room. The mess attendants were present in the mess room when the officers read and discussed the papers. In case of a great difference between my published reports and the tales brought forward by the mess attendants the men would conclude that I was purposely holding back something and that conditions in Germany were even worse than I stated them to be. And that, above all things, had to be avoided. So I told the crew that I would read the newspapers to them, word for word, reserving my comments until later on.

In order to characterize the business of Reuter's Bureau *in puncto* love of the truth, I found that their telegram, which we picked up in early August in the China Sea came in very handily. It said: "Official, *Emden* sunk in battle with *Askold*!"

Among none of my men could there exist the slightest uncertainty that this was a wild exaggeration, and I could always point to this telegram when estimating the truth of the other similar reports.

The men quickly learned the proper value to be placed on English reports.

Much pleasure was caused by a chart of Germany, on which the English had already "divided the skins of the bears." On this chart, France reached to Weser-Werra and to the Bavarian boundary, Denmark to the line of Wismar, Wittenberg, Magdeburg, Hanover, Bremen. England had swallowed up Oldenburg and Hanover. East of the Elbe, including Saxony, was, in the future, to be a part of the Empire of the Little Father. Bavaria remained an independent state. Of the German Empire there remained but one small spot called "Thüringen."

As soon as this was known, our men from Bavaria and Thüringen carried their heads especially high. In the first place, because they were regarded as important even to foreigners, and in the second place, because they believed themselves to be the pivots of the whole Empire.

How we did laugh about this!

The men took great pleasure in the daily hour in which they were read to. As soon as we had captured a steamer, and a bundle of newspapers arrived aboard, then in the next few hours all eyes seemed to say: "When will the reading commence?" Then followed the arguments among themselves as to who should stand watch, as no one wished to miss the reading. And, when the word was passed, "All hands aft," a yell of delight spread over the ship from the bow to the stern.

When the newspapers were being read, and though possibly the war reports were not very startling, still an energetic questioning always followed. Especially did they want to know about the ships of the squadron.

The battle of Santa Marie (Coronel), where for the first time in over a hundred years, an English squadron was defeated by an enemy of the same strength, naturally aroused the greatest enthusiasm. Everyone knew that the fate of the remaining ships of the squadron was as effectually sealed as was our own fate. Therefore, the happiness and pride was especially great to know that our armored cruisers had won the first German victory and had humbled an English squadron for the first time in over a hundred years.

Our work consisted mainly in making necessary repairs to the hull, machinery, and armament. In order to keep the crew fresh and clean, we rigged up a number of showers on deck, made out of old piping. Three times daily the entire crew was ordered to the showers, where each man could remain as long as he pleased.

The health of the men aboard the *Emden* was excellent. From the time we left Tsingtao until the final battle, we had not one single case of sickness. In the afternoons the ship's band played for quite a long time. The men sat around comfortably on the deck, forming a circle around the band, some dancing, smoking, or joining in with song. Usually in the evenings after dark, a glee club of good and strong singers would gather and render all the "possible" and "impossible" songs.

The "possible" songs were usually our beautiful German national songs, which were rendered excellently. The "impossible" songs were often composed as the singer went along. These usually consisted in trying to bring out clearly some idea or other; but rhyme and rhythm were neglected. The concluding air was always "The Watch on the Rhine," in which all hands who happened to be on deck always joined.

An unusual celebration always accompanied the business of "dividing the loot." From the captured steamers we took, always justly, everything that could be used aboard the *Emden*, especially edibles. And so a high mountain of provisions always piled up in its designated place on the quarterdeck. Sausages and hams hung suspended from the engine-room skylight. Mountains of chocolate and confections, bottles marked "Claret" and "Cognac," with three stars, ornamented the waterways. Live-stock was placed in its proper pen, accompanied by much grunting, squeaking, bleating, cackling, or quacking. The steward and his men made up a list. When all was ready the business of dividing was begun. The men, standing around in a large circle, smoking and chattering, had to spend a good deal of time in storing the allotted tasty-bits up forward after the dividing had finished.

In order to keep pace with the constant supply of provisions special meals were served. Chocolate or bonbons were served with coffee. Over 250,000 cigarettes were consumed by the smokers, and each evening, after the issue of "smokes," the deck seemed to be alive with hundreds of fire-flies. English flour, of which we received great quantities, gave the bakers all sorts of work. Excellent bread was made. Because of the bountiful supply of food stuffs, it became necessary for the officers to pay especial attention in guarding against over-feeding, instead of underfeeding.

It is unnecessary to state that we also brought aboard useful supplies of a nature other than provisions. Whenever I betook myself aboard a captured steamer I always carried along a request-list. Seldom did it happen that the requests were not filled. Even when the men requested such unusual things as soldering lamps, piassava brooms, rubber discs, file handles, dark lanterns, iron bars, fire-bricks, machine oil, etc. The men whom I took along over with me to bring back the stuff knew best what the men aboard ship wanted of those things which were at hand and not on the request-list. But among these I could not grant all the requests. I had to refuse permission to take aboard such articles as oil paintings, large mirrors, children's drums, live horses, etc.

At times when we thanked our stars for these things we could not but feel very sorry for our pursuers whom we knew to be close to us, and yet of whom we could say that they had had to live on hardtack and corned beef for weeks at a time, and that to them such things as beer, wine, cognac, fresh eggs, fried chicken, juicy ham, chocolate, bonbons, and cigarettes, must be "Fata Morgana" in their deluded dreams of their last port.

And so we passed our lives while the certain death's ring surrounded us, 16 cruisers uselessly burning their coals, and fruitlessly cudgeling their brains, in trying to catch us. As previously mentioned, when the enemy trade ceased and the captain decided to lay the *Emden* up for a short time, especially in order to clean her bottom, we steamed to the southward out of the Bay of Bengal region, until one fine day our anchor was dropped into the mud for the first time in a long, long while. We lay in the harbor of Diego Garcia. This is a small English island well down in the southern part of the Indian Ocean.

We had hardly anchored when the English flag was hoisted ashore. A boat containing an old Englishman approached us. Cheered by the sight of another human being, the old man came aboard with gifts of fish, eggs, vegetables, etc. He said he was much pleased to again for the first time in many years, greet his dear, beloved German brothers. He always loved to associate with Germans, especially aboard their wonderful warships. The last time he had done this was in 1889 when the German frigates *Bismarck* and *Marie* were in the harbor. And so he was now particularly pleased to see us, hoping that soon hereafter another German ship would anchor in Diego Garcia.

At first we were rather astonished at his greeting, even though we had previously experienced many peculiarities of the English. But soon we drew from him the fact that Diego Garcia receives mail but twice a year from Mauritius. Therefore, these people had not yet heard of the war. We did not have the heart to throw a scare into these folks, so we did not tell them. Why should we? Perhaps we would again visit there! When our guest arrived on deck, instead of seeing the usual beautiful snow-white decks of a German man-of-war, he saw a mess covered with oil stains and coal dust and with bare and scratched spots; and when he saw that our engine-room skylights were more of a black than a gray, that the rail was broken and torn away in many places, that only a few isolated patches of linoleum remained, that plaited matting (cargo nets) was hung around the guns as a splinter protection, that many spots on the bulkhead showed, where formerly something had been secured against them, and when he noticed that we had no more furniture in our mess room, his face took on a look of astonishment as he asked why all this was. We quieted him. We were in the middle of a world cruise. One had to leave such things behind and use every nook and cranny for coal storage. As for the rest, we gave him so much whiskey to drink that he gave up thinking. That, however, was not a hard thing for him to do. Laboriously he managed to make one request; would we please take the knocks out of his old, excessively vibrating motor-boat which had been there for the last six months? We promised him and fulfilled the promise.

The stay in the harbor was utilized in putting the ship in good condition, in cleaning and painting her and in scraping her bottom. The last could only be done in a very incomplete way and was done by flooding some compartments on one side, thus listing the ship. The opposite side, with part of her bottom exposed, was then scraped, the men working alongside in boats.

The stay in the harbor also gave us some hunting. Two objects which were seen floating in the water around the ship were taken for balls of old, dirty clothes thrown overboard from the ship, until suddenly these objects began to move and the lower edge appeared to be a light, shimmering silver. On closer approach they were discovered to be enormous rays (skates). I estimated them to be four to five square meters. They had large, wide, pale-colored mouths and were chasing smaller fish. Rifles were quickly brought on deck and we shot these animals. To do this one had to wait for the proper moment, when it happened to lift its flat back slightly out of the water. One lucky shot struck one of the animals in the back. He sprang up with a loud noise in a roll about 20 to 30 centimeters high, thrashing about madly with his broad flappers, so that he looked like a large bird in its death struggle.

Unfortunately we were unable to secure the beast.

Of course, the ship not being underway, much time was spent in fishing. All over the ship and out of all air ports hung the fishing lines and a rich catch was made in the harbor. The most curious forms were caught. All the colors were represented. Red, green, and blue fish of broad or narrow forms, with eyes above and eyes below, with or without scales. Every possible kind was brought aboard. The doctor inspected all the fish before they were eaten in order to keep from eating any of the poisonous varieties.

There were also some snakes. Unfortunately none were caught. They were about two meters long and of a pale green appearance. They would jump up out of the water and then swish their tails back and forth very rapidly, keeping their bodies almost vertical, and propel themselves along above the surface of the water at great speed.

This idyl unfortunately could last but a short time. Soon the *Emden* got underway, bound to perform new deeds. The region near the island of Minokoi yielded many more prizes.

In the meantime the regular steamer trade had started up again. We were especially touched by having the English Admiralty send us another fine, 7000-ton steamer laden with the best English-Welsh coal. But soon thereafter no more steamers came near Minokoi. Either the trade had ceased again or the ships were taking a different course. We were able to solve this later on.

Next, we took up the search to the northward of Minokoi. And see, after a short time, we fell in with an English steamer whose captain could say nothing except to ask this astonishing question: "Tell me, please, how did you find out the new secret courses prescribed by the Admiralty for merchant vessels?" That was the sign for us to expect more to pass this way. And so it did happen. In this way we made for the second time, the acquaintance of an English woman. The first thing that struck me was the way she took her fate. She amiably prattled around on deck giving cigarettes and chocolates to the men. According to her story it was evident that this interruption of her travels by the *Emden* was nothing new to her. First, while sailing from Hong Kong for Europe, her ship was turned back in the China Sea and she had to waste several weeks in Hong Kong because it was said that the *Emden* was about. Then she managed to get to Singapore and expected to start out again from there. Here again, while in the outer harbor, her ship was called back because the *Emden* was there. After several more wasted weeks of waiting she went from Singapore to Colombo, and on the outward journey from Colombo, she really did make our acquaintance. She returned to India on our "lucky bag."

Capturing a steamer at night was not an easy matter for

the *Emden*, and, at the same time, rather strenuous on the crew. We never knew whether the approaching vessel was a warship or not. Unless, beyond the shadow of a doubt, it was definitely known that we were dealing with a merchantman, we had to call the crew to their battle stations. Also we had to reckon on the possibility of the English having warships convoying their merchantmen. The man-of-war would then steam along a short distance behind the merchantman, and, while the *Emden* was devoting her attention to the steamer, the warship would suddenly and unexpectedly attack us.

One time we thought we were confronted by a warship. It was a dark night. A steamer, lights burning, came toward us. Evidently a merchantman. We, totally darkened of course, approached her from dead ahead. Just as we were about to turn on her, we saw behind her a dark body. It might have been a darkened warship. We could not tell what it was. Therefore we started to attack.

"Both engines full speed ahead. Torpedo-tubes ready! At him!"

On near approach we had, it must be admitted, directed our attack at a smoke cloud which, by chance, the steamer had made at this place and which, due to the dead calm, had hung close to the water.

Unfortunately, we did not escape from often meeting neutral ships in this neighborhood. After an examination we had to let them go again. All of these were Hollanders.

We were very pleased that the Hollanders behaved themselves better than the *Loredano* did on a previous occasion. We never intercepted a radio from a Hollander in which the *Emden* was mentioned. At another time we proved that the Dutchmen, in order to observe strict neutrality, forbade their vessels sending out miscellaneous war news by radio. We caught one radio in which an English ship requested a Dutch ship to signal her the reports from the war. The answer said: "We are not allowed to radio war news."

And so did the *Emden* cruise about in a very small part of

the ocean, chased by 16 more-powerful pursuers, and all the
time naturally confined to the regular steamer tracks. Because
there, and there only, could prizes be expected.

Because of the inability of the enemy to catch us and because the *Emden* struck like lightning, bobbing up here and
then there, the English-Indian newspapers published a yarn
that there were several German ships about, and they all bore
the same name.

Soon we were no longer called the *Emden*, but "The Flying
Dutchman."

CHAPTER 5

Fire Baptized

MERCHANTMEN AGAIN FAILED TO COME, and as the *Emden* had just finished overhauling, we had to plan something else to fill in the present pause. After much reflection, the captain decided that our enemies from Colombo and Singapore must have a rendezvous where they could coal, provision, and rest their men. The most likely advance base seemed to be the harbor of Penang. According to the press reports we concluded that the French armored cruisers *Montcalm* and *Dupleix*, especially, would frequent this place. These or any other ships would, said the captain, be attacked in their own harbor.

The night of October 27–28 found the *Emden* before Penang, heading in toward the harbor at high speed. The captain wished to enter with the first gray streaks of daylight. Navigating the narrow harbor entrance by night is too dangerous. Also, early morning seems to be the time of soundest sleep, and a surprise attack at that hour promised the best hope of success. At the proper time, all hands on the *Emden* were aroused. The ship was absolutely "cleared for action," that means, she was made ready in all respects for a battle. The

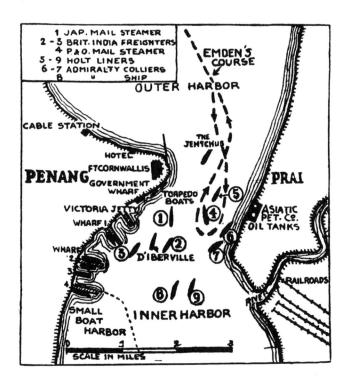

men were served a good warm breakfast. Clean linen and clean clothes were donned in order to avoid chances of infecting any wounds.

Totally darkened, steaming without making any smoke, each man at his station, the ship approached the enemy harbor. It was shortly before sunrise. The night was dark. But, in low latitudes, the rising of the sun means immediate and full daylight. Several small, harmless fishing vessels were passed close-to in the darkness of the night near the harbor and only the watchfulness of the officer of the deck, who turned out of his course, prevented their being run down.

Close to the harbor entrance we saw on our port side a bright white light that showed for about a second and then suddenly disappeared. It was most certainly an electric light, evidently on an outpost or watch-keeping boat. The ship itself was not sighted. But its mere presence led us to suspect that some warships were in the harbor. Naturally, the fourth smokepipe that had often rendered such good service was set up on the *Emden*.

As our ship arrived off the inner reefs of Penang, the first faint streaks of daylight began to show over the dark mountains ashore. We had arrived at exactly the proper time. In the short prevailing twilight we could see a large number of ships in the harbor. To all appearances, only merchantmen. No matter how hard we strained our eyes we could see nothing that resembled a man-of-war. We had already begun to think that we had made a failure of it, when suddenly, in the middle of the undarkened merchant ships, we saw something that was both dark and darkened. All eyes for a man-of-war. After a few minutes we were close enough aboard to make certain that it was some sort of warship. Soon we saw three white lights, equal distances apart, in the midst of the darkened, black mass. Our first thoughts were: these are the stern lights of three destroyers moored alongside each other. Soon we discovered, however, that this assumption was not correct. The ship's hull, now coming into plain sight, was much too large for a destroyer. The enemy ship was swinging to the tide with her stern toward us, so that unfortunately she did not make a silhouette. Not until the *Emden* had passed within about 200 meters from her stern, the enemy being abeam of us, could we definitely identify the vessel as the *Zemtchug*. Peace and quiet reigned on her. We had arrived so close aboard that we could distinctly recognize the Russian cruiser in the early gray of morning. We could not see the officer of the deck, nor the lookouts, nor even a signal watch. At a distance of 200 meters our first torpedo flew out of the starboard broadside tube, and at the same time our broadside guns opened up into the forecastle of the *Zemtchug* where the crew was asleep. The torpedo hit the enemy cruiser in the stern. One could plainly see the tremor that ran through the ship when she was struck. The stern was lifted about a quarter to a half meter out of the water and then the ship immediately began to settle slowly by the stern. The Russians now began showing signs of life. The doors, leading from the officers' rooms on deck, were torn from their hinges. Many officers came running but seemed to know their way to their battle stations very imperfectly. Without tarrying very long to consider, they hurried aft to the flagstaff and hopped overboard. A long row of sailors followed suit. Evidently these were their servant-boys, who follow their masters through thick and thin.

In the meantime our guns carried on a rapid fire, at point blank range, into the *Zemtchug*. The *Emden* steamed past the enemy cruiser at very slow speed at a distance of 400 meters. The broadsides continued raining shells into her. The fore part of the ship was riddled in a few minutes. A fierce fire was eating up the forecastle. One could look clear through the ship through the large holes in her sides. One after another the projectiles kept on hitting. When they hit you could see a sharp, pale flash. Then, after a few seconds, as if flaming hoops were whirling around the spot where it hit, it reached the inside of the ship and then exploded, shooting the smoke out through the holes in the side meters in size. I did not see a single man escape from the forward part of the *Zemtchug*.

Meantime the *Emden* was being fired on from three sides. Where the shells came from we did not know. We merely heard the whistling of the shells and then saw them strike the merchant-men that lay around us. Even the *Zemtchug* woke up and opened fire. As her guns were larger than ours, a hit on us could have resulted disastrously. Even though the *Emden* might not be put out of the fight, still she could receive such damage that, not having a means of making repairs, her activities would have been considerably curtailed. The captain, therefore, ordered a second torpedo to be fired.

The *Emden* having passed the *Zemtchug*, was turned around to port by means of her engines, and then started again to pass by her enemy. The second torpedo left the tube at 400 meters range. It had become so light that we could clearly see the air-bubble trail of this shot. After a few seconds there followed a powerful detonation in the neighborhood of the navigating bridge of the Russian cruiser. A giant, black smoke cloud, mixed with gray smoke, white steam, and spray, rose to a height of about 150 meters. Parts of the ship were torn off and flew around in the air. We could see the cruiser break in half. Bow and stern went under. Then the explosion cloud covered everything over, and, after it had cleared away, about 10 to 15 seconds later, there remained nothing more to be seen of the cruiser except the truck of her mast.[1]

The water where the ship sank was filled with floating wreckage and swimming men. The *Emden* did not have to bother about the swimmers. There were many fishing boats in this neighborhood who could readily rescue all the men.

We ceased firing in the meantime. The other two places that were firing at us also ceased. We still could not determine from whence came the shells.

Soon we saw the French gunboat *D'Iberville* lying at anchor, hidden among the merchant vessels. Evidently that was one of the places from which we were fired on. The captain had

---

1. As a result of a court martial held August 21–25 at Vladivostok over the loss of the Russian cruiser *Jemtchug*, the following verdict was presented:

The captain of the ship, Baron Tscherkassof, was found guilty of the following negligence: He had been in command of the *Jemtchug* since June 14, 1914. On August 25, 1914, he left Vladivostok for the scene of hostilities, where he was to place himself under the direction of the British Admiral Jerome. In spite of the fact that he was on war service, he had given the order that in case of smoke or lights on the horizon no general call should be given; he had not seen to it that the crew should sleep at regular hours; at night he had not increased the number on duty; he had not put torpedos in readiness for an engagement; on entering harbor he had given orders to put the ship out of war trim; during the ship's stay in port he had allowed her to lie at anchor with open lights; with only an anchor watch, and with strangers at liberty to visit the ship and look her over freely.—*Norddeutsche Allgemeine Zeitung*, 1/10.

just given the order to turn to port in order to pass the wreck of the *Zemtchug* and head for the *D'Iberville*, when the lookouts reported an enemy destroyer standing in. We could not permit her to attack us in the narrow confines of the harbor. It was impossible to maneuver in here so as to avoid a torpedo shot. Therefore the captain turned toward the destroyer at full speed in order to engage her in the outer and larger part of the harbor. We could plainly see the craft heading straight for us. The high, narrow bow, the low, broad smokepipes behind, coming at us at high speed. She seemed to be a typical English destroyer of a large type.

At 4000 meters we opened fire on her. High splashes where our shells hit arose all around and close aboard her. Then the vessel turned hard to starboard. It became evident that she was a fairly large English government steamer. The mirage that is especially strong just at sunrise, had so distorted the appearance of the ship that she seemed to be exactly like a destroyer. We ceased firing immediately.

On coming about in order to attack the *D'Iberville* once more, it was reported that a large merchantman was standing in. Even at a considerable distance we could make her out to be a merchant vessel. The captain then decided to capture her next. The *D'Iberville* could not escape us anyway. Our cutter was quickly lowered. The steamer received the usual signal, "Stop, we are sending a boat!" But hardly had our cutter gone alongside the steamer when we again saw a warship heading in from sea. Therefore we recalled and hoisted the cutter, and headed for our new opponent.

The mirage this morning seemed to be exceptional. The form of the oncoming ship changed every second. At first she appeared to be a large black ship, with smokepipes fore and aft. Without doubt, a man-of-war. Then she suddenly seemed to shrink. Half of the smokepipes disappeared, and she then appeared to be a small gray merchantman with black rings around her smokepipes. A few minutes later she changed her form once more. She had become very small, very black, and with two smokepipes. Therefore, we finally decided that she was a warship of some sort, probably a French destroyer. Now, up and at her!

The *Emden* at this time flew no flag. Neither did the approaching vessel. When about 6000 meters away the on-comer hoisted the tri-color. So, now a Frenchman! She came toward us uncertainly and seemed throughout to fail to grasp who we were. What caused her to act like this is beyond me. She certainly must have heard the firing of the guns and the detonations of the torpedoes, and after that she might at least have expected to see a cruiser standing out of the harbor. In spite of that, she held her course passing us. When the range became 4000 meters we hoisted our battleflags. The *Emden* turned slightly to port, showed her our broadside and the first salvo was on its way toward her. And now the French ship knew with whom she had to deal. She turned hard to port, put on full speed and attempted to escape. Too late! The third salvo landed five hits on her quarterdeck. An explosion, evidently a magazine, a large cloud of black coal dust and white steam covered the entire after part of the ship. In spite of the evident stupidity of the French ship, we must give her credit for manning her battery very promptly. Two torpedoes were launched at the *Emden*, while the bow gun opened fire on us. The torpedoes did not reach their mark as the *Emden* was beyond torpedo range. They came up about 900 meters off our starboard beam. The bow gun fired only a very few shots before it was smothered under a hail of shell from our guns. Mast, smokepipe, forward tower, superstructure, ventilators, and all were knocked overboard. In a very few minutes she sank. She was the French destroyer *Mousquet*.

The captain stopped at the place where the ship had sunk. Both cutters were lowered and the live swimmers were picked up. Many of these floated about, some holding on to wooden wreckage, others, with life-belts on, strung out at great distances apart. This showed that the first men to jump overboard must have done so at the very beginning of the fight.

In the *Emden's* cutters were the doctor and such first-aid material as could hastily be collected. As our cutters approached the swimming Frenchmen they did the most remarkable thing, that is, they tried to swim away from the rescuing boats. The beach was so far away that it was impossible for them to swim that great distance. The reason for their fleeing from our boats came to light later on. We picked up 33 Frenchmen, some of them wounded, also one wounded officer. Thanks to the fact that we had our doctor ready to go along in the cutters, we managed to have two-thirds of the wounded all bandaged and splints adjusted ready to be hoisted aboard in hammocks by the time the boats returned alongside. Meanwhile another French torpedo-boat was seen to be standing out of the harbor and heading for us. It was high time for the *Emden* to get to sea. It seemed certain that other French and English men-of-war must be in the neighborhood. It was impossible for the unarmored *Emden* to successfully engage in a battle in broad daylight with more powerful warships. Therefore we proceeded to sea at high speed on a westerly course. The French destroyer followed us for some time, but finally disappeared into the rainbow and was never seen again. Our intention of drawing the destroyer out to sea after us, and then turning around and sinking her, was therefore not accomplished.

We did the best we could aboard ship to attend to the wounded and captured Frenchmen. The wounded were given medical attention in the sick bay. A large, firm, wood and canvas house was built up on the starboard side of the main deck, next the engine-room skylight, for the accommodation of the unwounded. We had in our crew two seamen who spoke French fluently. These were relieved from all duties and assigned as interpreters for the wounded in the sick bay and for the other prisoners on deck. We quickly hammered together a few benches and tables. Although our men had few clothes left, they voluntarily and willingly gave clothes to the prisoners, most of whom had arrived on board with very little on.

The prisoners were given food, drink, and smoking material. They were restricted as little as possible in their movements about the decks.

When we asked the Frenchmen why they swam away from our rescuing cutters they gave this answer: "In our newspapers we read that the Germans massacre all their prisoners. We, therefore, preferred drowning to being murdered. The officers also told us the same things which we had read in the newspapers."

On further questioning, when we asked how it happened that on the previous night they allowed the *Emden* to pass on into the harbor, they answered that they had seen the *Emden*. But, as we had four smokepipes, they thought we were the English cruiser *Yarmouth* and therefore did not hinder us. Most undoubtedly the white light that we sighted during the night off Penang must have been this French destroyer. They explained that their captain had both legs shot off by one of our shells. He could have been saved, but he lashed himself to the bridge in order to sink with his ship, because he did not care to live and face the shame of having had a part of his crew jump overboard at the very beginning of the fight. Hats off to an officer of this caliber!

Among the wounded there were three serious cases. Recovery was impossible. One died the first evening, and the two others the next day.

The first dead man was, according to the customs of the sea, sewed up in canvas and weighted, and lay in state on the starboard side of the quarterdeck. The corpse was covered with the French war flag. A sentry stood watch on this post throughout the night. The next morning the dead was buried from the starboard gangway. The ship was stopped during the ceremony. One division of the *Emden*'s seamen, in parade uniform, took part in the ceremonies. All the unwounded Frenchmen also took part. A guard of honor with rifles and commanded by an officer, attended. All the German officers, wearing service uniforms and their medals, were present. The captain spoke a sermon in French. Among other things he said that the departed had died with honor in the service of his country and that the enemy would not deny him any of the honorable ceremony which he deserved. Then followed a prayer, read from our Catholic prayer book, as the Frenchman was of that religion. As the corpse, covered with the French flag, disappeared into the deep, the guard of honor presented arms and then fired three volleys over the grave. The officers stood, at the salute, alongside the gangway. The same ceremonies were repeated the next day when the other two were buried.

After a few days we were able to transfer the Frenchmen to an English steamer whose neutral cargo we could not destroy. When they were told to prepare to leave the ship, the two eldest petty officers came to me with the request to see the captain. They gave the captain their thanks and the thanks of their comrades for the honorable and humane treatment and reception which they had received on board. They now knew that what their newspapers had said about the Germans were lies and they would do all they could when they reached home to spread the truth. Both these petty officers said the same to me.

The badly wounded officer, on leaving the ship, requested one of the *Emden* cap ribbons. He said that he wished to have a keepsake from a ship whose officers and men behaved in such a humane and honorable way to a wounded and defeated enemy.

We also transferred to the steamer a large quantity of medicinal supplies, so that the wounded would be properly taken care of. The steamer then received orders to proceed to Sabang in order to land the Frenchmen. The nearest hospital was at that place. Later on we read in the newspapers that unfortunately the wounded officer had died there.

The most ridiculous reports were made by the English in regard to the Penang battle. They complained that the *Emden* had approached the harbor under the English flag and for this reason was not recognized. They also said that the *Emden* had gone into the harbor by the southern entrance and had left by the northern entrance. These reports are groundless and untrue. In the first place the *Emden* never flew the English flag, and further it was night when the *Emden* came in. The carrying of a flag therefore would have served no purpose. The southern entrance to Penang is so shallow that the *Emden* could not possibly have entered that way. The only thing in the English reports worth attention is the praise devoted to our captain, referring to our picking up the Frenchmen after the *Mousquet* sank.

Here again was shown the knightly conduct of the *Emden*'s captain, the conduct which he repeatedly exhibited in his meteoric career during the war. As the French torpedo-boats might have dashed out any time, every second was precious to him. Without considering for a minute his own danger, he stopped and sent out boats to pick up the remainder of the living of the *Mousquet* before he again proceeded on his way. As the report reads, "He played the game."

Further, I will permit myself to quote the following words, "And so ended this engagement that will forever remain as an historical example of the possibility of two ships, approximately of the same power, engaging in battle in broad daylight at the shortest possible range, without both of them being totally destroyed. A case such as that which occurred yesterday, has always been considered by all naval authorities as either impossible or a case of suicide."

The authorities evidently referred to men other than those under the command of our captain.

CHAPTER 6

Our Daily Bread

THE PRINCIPAL CONSIDERATION ABOARD our ship was the providing of coal. The collier *Markomannia* had devotedly followed us on our cruise from Tsingtao to the southward into the Indian Ocean. The supply of coal practically ceased when our presence in the Indian Ocean became known. There were no harbors into which we could run to get fuel. We therefore had to earn our daily bread. And then we had the good luck to take, as our first prize, the collier *Pontoporros*, which brought us several thousand tons of coal. But, as I said before, her coal was of such an inferior quality that it could not be used except in case of urgent need. For a while we tested the *Pontoporros* coal. A heavy, black, treacherous mountain of smoke hung over the ship. The boilers choked with soot and were reduced in efficiency. The whole deck was always covered with a fine rain of unburned or partly burned cinders. The dirty coal dust penetrated through all crevices and into all air ports. In short, everybody prayed for a better quality of coal.

We took more pleasure in capturing that steamer containing several thousand tons of excellent Welsh coal than we would have taken in capturing a ship full of gold.

The *Emden* was constantly being coaled. We had to have a large quantity of coal on board in case we had an action forced on us. Therefore, we never permitted our amount of coal on hand to drop below a certain percentage. And so the coaling of the *Emden* became almost a daily performance—our daily bread.

Coaling ship is not an easy or pleasant job for the crew. The tropical heat made itself felt. Especially in the bunkers, where the firemen had to trim the coal, the temperature was often unbearable. While coaling, wearing apparel was reduced to mere nothing. The so-called "coaling-packages," that is, the old and worn outfits which are worn only when coaling ship, were soon in a poor state of repair due to their constant use. We could not get other clothes to replace these. The trousers, which were originally of the regular length, gradually came through at the calf and then at the knee. After a time the long trousers became short ones, a little later the short ones became bathing trunks, and again a little later—of this, I will not tell! I need only remark that the uncovered parts were soon hidden by coal dust. We had to coal at sea. A constant and appreciable swell runs in the Indian Ocean at all times. The ships never ceased rolling. Never was the operation entirely free from danger.

We used so-called fenders to protect the ships when coming alongside each other. These are heavily plaited mats or balls of roping. They are used to protect the ships and prevent the heavy rubbing of one against the other. Due to the excessive rolling of the *Emden* and her colliers, the fenders soon wore out. We also discovered that they were not sufficiently large to stand the operation of coaling at sea. So we had to get to work making new ones.

Before leaving Tsingtao I took 150 hammocks along. Originally my idea was to use them for stopping leaks. In case of injury below water, hammocks can be used to plug up the holes and thereby reduce the amount of water streaming in.

The hammocks now came in handy. We made great, long

fenders in which we secured heavy logs about four to six meters long, and suspended them along the sides of the ship. The fenders were usually pretty well used up by the time each coaling was finished; but new ones could be made ready for the next coaling.

One of the best fenders of that style was made of automobile tires, a great number of which we took from one of our prizes. All along the sides we hung these tires and they made most excellent buffer cushions.

Coaling at sea is at best a tedious business. The two ships, tied up side by side, always rolled quite heavily. When the coal bags were hoisted up to the tops of the coaling booms we had to wait some time until the proper moment when the ships rolled toward each other. Then the falls were let go and the coal bags landed any old place on the *Emden*'s deck. The men had to learn to spring aside at the proper moment in order to save themselves.

The constant surging of the vessels against each other and the heaving of the heavy coal bags on the *Emden*'s decks caused no little damage, as you may well imagine. We always coaled on the starboard side of the ship. The *Emden* had a swallow's nest forward and aft in each of which a gun was mounted. (Sponsons.) When the ships rolled together the forward sponson was always in danger and had, at various times, been crushed in. The main sight was attached to the left side of the gun. When we coaled on the starboard side it was impossible to damage the main gun-sight.

The auxiliary gun-sight, which was secured at the right side of the gun (outboard) was crushed after a short time. The gun-shutters of the sponson had been crushed in by a collision with the collier and smashed against the gun.

The coal bags constantly struck the rail. Soon there remained not one single whole stanchion along the whole starboard side. The linoleum deck received rough treatment. As a result one could see the steel deck through the large holes. However, that did not harm the deck very much. But the exposed deck was so slippery that the men constantly fell, especially at night or when the ship rolled. Whenever we finished coaling we proceeded to roughen up the slippery spots, that is, we cut small grooves in the deck, so that it would furnish a better foothold. Then, when we managed to get a supply of canvas and tar from some of the English ships, we covered up the exposed steel deck.

As I said before, the *Emden* had to have as much coal aboard as possible all the time. Therefore, we not only kept the bunkers full, but also carried a deck load. Forward on the port side, amidships next the engine-room skylight, and aft on the poop, we piled mountains of coal. Communication about the ship was naturally made rather difficult. If we wanted to get along on the upper deck, it became necessary to squeeze through narrow passageways between piles of coal as high as a man's head. Frequently it also happened that the heavy roll would cause the coal to slide and then the whole deck was scattered full of it.

Coal dust and coal dirt was found all over the ship. Whenever we had a deck load we would strike as much as we possibly could down into the bunkers the first thing after reveille each day. The wooden deck suffered a great deal by the constant dragging of the heavy coal bags. Deep, dirty grooves were worn in the wood. Oil stains were to be seen everywhere. Of course, the paint work itself was ruined. No one who had seen the *Emden* before would have recognized her now as being the same ship, for when she was cruising the East Asiatic station she was known as the "Swan of the East" because her condition always appeared to be above reproach.

Our enemies had always thought it was impossible to coal in the open ocean. They evidently were judging from their own standard of seamanship. We heard that they were constantly searching for us in all the quiet harbors and hidden anchorages in the hope that they would some day catch us coaling in one of those places. Instead, rolling peacefully, we were coaling at sea.

I can still see the troubled and questioning face of the English captain of our prize *Buresk*—he had, as said, gone over into our service—when, during a period of heavy rolling, the *Buresk* received the signal, "Prepare to coal." He assumed this to be impossible and thought that both ships would be wrecked. About six or eight hours later he had to admit that the seamanship in the German Navy is not the slightest bit disturbed by heavy rolling or a strong seaway.

The coaling always took a fairly long time. In spite of that the *Emden* had right fair success. When the weather was unfavorable we used to take on about 40 tons per hour. But we also had times when the weather improved a bit. Then we would average 70 tons per hour. Whoever has coaled from a collier at sea will readily admit that this was a good record.

We coaled alternately from the *Buresk* and *Exford*. Although the *Emden* did not entirely escape injury, due to the continuous rolling, still our greatest anxiety was the fear that the colliers could not stand it. They were brand new ships, built in England, and making their maiden voyages. But they were so lightly and poorly constructed that at the conclusion of every coaling they bore great indentations along their sides. Regular trash!

Those hours when the *Emden* had a collier alongside and was busily engaged in coaling were very dangerous ones for us. The ship was not cleared for action. We knew that the circle of death surrounded us. Any moment an enemy might appear over the horizon and attack us. In that case we would be obliged to make many preparations before we were ready. During the coaling it was imperative that the guns be kept covered over. Likewise they had to be run in because they projected from the side and might have been injured (by the collier). Therefore, it was always necessary to finish coaling as soon as possible. The men also understood this and put forth their greatest efforts.

The work was lightened as much as possible. The steward prepared huge tubs of lemonade up forward. The mixture was cooled off by the addition of ice. Can after can was filled with lemonade and carried to the working men. The band played lively airs. A large bulletin board was set up amidships so as to be visible from all around. Each quarter hour the amount of coal received was chalked up on the board. The figures were quoted for each ship's watch. Neither watch would admit the superiority of the other. They eagerly noted the increases of the other watch and then, by doubling their efforts, attempted to break the record.

High up in the tops sat the lookouts, armed with binoculars, and with wide-awake eyes searched the horizon for possible smoke clouds or mast heads.[1]

ITINERARY OF *EMDEN*

Location	1914	Remarks
Yellow Sea	August 2	Outbreak of war
Tsingtao (arrrived)	August 5*	
Tsingtao (left)	August 7	
Met fleet, probably at Lamo-trek Island (Caroline group)	August 12	
Entered Bay of Bengal	September 4*	Route uncertain, Aug. 12–Sept. 4
Off Calcutta, India	September 10–14	
Off Rangoon	September 18*	
Madras	September 22	Bombardment
Off Colombo	September 30	
Diego Garcia	October 5–10*	
Off Minokoi Island	October 15–20	
Penang	October 28	Sank *Zemtchug* and *Mousquet*
Straits of Sunda	November 1–6*	
Keeling, Cocos Island	November 9	Destroyed by Australian cruiser *Sydney*

*Indicates approximate dates.

1. Translator's Note.—A study of the accompanying chart and of the itineraries of the *Emden* and of her landing party, and also of the table of vessels sunk by the *Emden*, will accurately locate the scenes of all operations.

EMDEN'S VICTIMS

Date	Name	Voyage	Cargo	Value	Tonnage	Remarks
Aug. 3, 1914	Rjesan	Hong Kong to Vladivostok	Passenger Steamer		3,522	Taken to Tsingtao. Converted into auxiliary cruiser under name of *Cormoran*. Later on interned at Guam
Sept. 10, 1914	Pontoporros		Coal		4,049	Captured. Recaptured by English cruiser *Yarmouth*
Sept. 10, 1914	Indus	Calcutta to England	General	$ 690,000	3,393	Sunk
Sept. 11, 1914	Lovat	Calcutta to Bombay	Ballast	300,000	6,102	Sunk
Sept. 12, 1914	Cabinga				4,657	Captured. Loaded with crews of other ships and then let go
Sept. 13, 1914	Killin	Calcutta to Colombo	Coal	215,000	3,544	Sunk
Sept. 13, 1914	Diplomat	Calcutta to England	General	1,500,000	7,615	Sunk
Sept. 14, 1914	Trabboch	Negapatam to Calcutta	Ballast	100,000	4,014	Sunk
Sept. 14, 1914	Clan Matheson			190,000	4,775	Sunk
Sept. 25–30, 1914	King Lud	Alexandria to Calcutta	Ballast	200,000	3,650	Sunk
Sept. 25–30, 1914	Tymeric	Samarang to Falmouth	General	655,000	3,314	Sunk
Sept. 27–30, 1914	Foyle	From Sfax	Ballast	150,000	4,147	Sunk 315 miles off Colombo
Sept. 27–30, 1914	Riberia	Alexandria to Batavia	Ballast	150,000	4,147	Sunk 200 miles west of Colombo
*Sept. 30, 1914	Buresk	From Port Said	Coal	160,000	4,350	Captured. After defeat of *Emden*, *Buresk* sunk by own crew before *Sydney* could capture her
Sept. 30, 1914	Gryfedale				4,437	Captured and released

EMDEN'S VICTIMS (continued)

Date	Name	Voyage	Cargo	Value	Tonnage	Remarks
Oct. 15–20, 1914	Clan Grant	Great Britain to Calcutta	General	640,000	3,948	Sunk
Oct. 16–20, 1914	Ben Mohr	Great Britain to Far East	General	815,000	4,806	Sunk
Oct. 16–20, 1914	Ponrabbel (Dredger)	Great Britain to Launceston	Ballast	145,000	473	Sunk
Oct. 18–20, 1914	Troilus	Yokohama to Great Britain	General	3,400,000	7,562	Sunk
Oct. 18–20, 1914	Chilkana	Great Britain to Calcutta	General	1,060,000	5,146	Sunk
Oct. 20, 1914	Exford	From Cardiff	Coal	275,000	4,542	Captured. Recaptured by *Empress of Japan* and sunk off Padang
Oct. 20, 1914	St. Egbert				5,596	Captured. Loaded with crews of other ships and then let go
Oct. 28, 1914	Zemtchug	At anchor in Penang	Russian Cruiser		3,130	Sunk by two torpedoes and gun fire
Oct. 28, 1914	Mousquet	Off Penang	French Destroyer		298	Sunk by gun fire

Markomannia, Emden's tender, was sunk by English cruiser *Yarmouth.*
Buresk sunk by own crew before *Sydney* could capture her on Nov. 9, 1914. Took three officers, one warrant officer, and 12 men, prisoners.
A collier was sunk by the *Empress of Japan* off Padang. Probably *Exford.*
*Date uncertain.

When the coaling had reached the point where the collier could shove off, we turned-to on stowing the deck load. When that was finished we tried to get at least the thickest of the dirt clear of the sleeping places. Then the crew washed, took a shower and changed clothes. After this they had their supper, and shortly thereafter turned in. Very often it happened that the exhausted men had hardly gone to sleep when some steamer was sighted and then they had to be called on for several more hours of strenuous work.

No, it was not an easy life. No one, however, had any idea that it could be otherwise. One time, at my suggestion, the captain permitted a steamer to get away because I told him the men had just completed ten strenuous hours of coaling and had about reached the point of exhaustion. The next day, when this became known, a growling grumbling was heard: "We would have fixed that one too."

CHAPTER 7

The Distress of the Nibelungs

AFTER LEAVING PENANG THE captain decided to cruise to the southward. We imagined that all the trading ships in the Bay of Bengal would be held up in their harbors again for a considerable time. *Emden* herself had given definite notice of her presence in this region when she sank the *Zemtchug* and the *Mousquet*. Also we had to assume that the hunt for the *Emden* in the Bay of Bengal would now be more thorough than heretofore. Therefore it seemed that the Straits of Sunda gave more promise of success in capturing merchantmen. The cargo vessels coming from Australia hardly touched the waters around India; instead, when coming from the Straits of Sunda or from West Australia they proceed across the Indian Ocean straight toward Sokotra and then into the Red Sea.

The next thing was to find our collier *Buresk*. We left her outside of Penang. Due to her slow speed of barely 11 knots, she could not follow us during the engagement.

The *Buresk* was found at her previously appointed position. The news of the fight created the greatest excitement. And now, at the customary speed of 11 knots, we proceeded south. Soon we sighted the islands lying off the western coast of

Sumatra. As the main ships' route lay between Sumatra and the islands, the captain decided to remain in these straits. It was not so rough behind the islands as in the open sea. We could coal more readily. Further, we had reason to believe that the first warships to search these quiet waters would be English and Japanese torpedo-boat destroyers. It was not impossible that we might catch one or more of these.

Near the island of Sima-loer we coaled once more. The sea was so exceptionally calm that we speedily finished the job. The *Emden* was then about eight sea miles off the coast, well outside of neutral waters.

Soon a small fishing vessel, motor driven, came out from the beach and headed for us. It carried the flag of Holland at the masthead. A Dutch officer, who introduced himself as the commandant of the island, came aboard to ask if the *Emden* were not in neutral waters. In this case he requested us to go a little farther out. Whether that was the real reason for his visit, or whether he merely wanted to carry on a little conversation, I do not know. A mere estimate by eye would surely tell him that we were considerably more than three sea miles distant from the beach.

We asked him aboard. The captain also invited him to his cabin. He told us that Portugal had declared war on us. Evidently they did this for our special enjoyment. Good jokes were always welcome to us.

Unwittingly I had at first offended the commander of the island. When his boat came alongside, mistaking him for a fisherman, I asked if he had any fish for sale, which he indignantly resented. But this early misunderstanding did not mar our pleasant acquaintance. He seemed to enjoy himself in our mess room.

The *Emden* cruised about in the waters of Sunda Straits for some time. But nothing was sighted. Evidently, even in this region, all shipping had been entirely held up. Ordinarily, shipping is very active in the Sunda Straits.

For two months our ship had been cruising around among

enemies. I have previously said that everybody on board was now certain that the *Emden*'s operations could not continue much longer. Conditions were rapidly becoming worse. When we first entered the Bay of Bengal we knew that our enemies were not ready to thoroughly search for us and that there were few warships in the Indian Ocean. Most of their ships were after our armored cruisers in the Pacific Ocean. Soon, however, we read the reports in the newspapers and secured other information which showed us that a great number of more powerful ships were on our trail. Some of this information we received from the crews of the captured steamers.

Even the English-speaking Indians whom we captured on the steamers could speak of nothing but German defeats. Later on, however, they changed their opinions. One Indian, whom we questioned along about the end of September, said that the English newspapers contained nothing but German reverses. They also had Indian newspapers which printed articles substantially different. These papers were then suppressed by the English. But most of the Indians understood that England was not as successful as the English claimed. They were greatly pleased by this, and said: "England by-and-by finished."

Another Indian told us a characteristic story. He said that two English cruisers with two smoke-pipes and two masts always remained at Colombo. One of these was always on watch at sea, and, when relieved by the other, returned to port, etc. One day one of these cruisers returned with only one mast and one smoke-pipe, many wounded aboard, and the ship pretty well shot up. The other cruiser never returned again. Is this perhaps one of the cases where the *Emden* was destroyed?

A Chinese, coming from Hong Kong, said that one day two Japanese cruisers, severely injured by gunfire and filled up with many wounded, came into Hong Kong. *Emden* did not take part in this sea-fight, nor, as we now know, did the other ships of the German squadron.

All in all, the *Emden* was being pursued most thoroughly. The moment when her game would be played out was not far distant. The spirit of the entire ship, however, was for keeping on going. If one should come he would soon see with whom he had to reckon.

As no more ships were sighted in the Straits of Sunda, the captain decided to destroy the radio and cable station on Keeling Island. The cable connection between Australia and the home country had long since been destroyed by the other vessels of our squadron. Keeling was the last direct connection between Australia and England. Should this be destroyed, the only other connection would be via the neutral Dutch cable in the East Indies. We therefore assumed that England had made some preparation to protect their last station. It would have been an easy matter to transport several hundred men to Keeling and prevent a landing by the *Emden*'s landing force. The only thing the *Emden* could do was to destroy the station with her heavy guns. But this would not accomplish much. Especially would the cables have escaped. And as for the small apparatus needed on land, a reserve instrument could have been rigged up in a few minutes, and several hours after the destruction of the building the telegraphing could have been started up again. Also the English might have known that in case the island were attacked by the *Emden* they would not have to fear a long bombardment. The captain would have to save his ammunition for other purposes, instead of wasting it on the superficial destruction of the telegraph service.

As we had to reckon on resistance, we made all possible preparations in order that the landing force would be as powerful as we could make it. The four machine guns were taken along. A force of 50 men was equipped. In addition to the machine guns, the offensive equipment consisted of 29 rifles and 24 revolvers. It was impossible for the *Emden*, with her small complement, to land more than 50 men. We had previously, out of our own crew, manned the prizes *Pontoporros, Exford* and *Buresk*, and several men were also on the *Markomannia*.

During the night of November 8–9, 1914, the *Emden* and her tender *Buresk* were 50 sea miles west of Keeling. The collier *Exford* had been sent to another rendezvous in the ocean. It was possible that an English cruiser might be found at anchor in the harbor of Keeling. Then there was the danger of having the *Buresk* sighted and captured, while the *Emden*, returning after the completion of her task, would have to run the risk of escaping from a stronger cruiser. If she escaped she would then find her other collier at some point out of the sight of the enemy.

Buresk received orders during the night to remain 50 sea miles west of the island and not to come to Keeling unless she received orders by radio. The captain intended, in case everything went off smoothly and after the destruction of the station, to coal in Keeling Harbor.

At sunrise on the morning of November 9 the *Emden* was close to the entrance to Port Refuge, the anchorage of the island of Keeling. The difficult channel through the reefs was found. *Emden* anchored. The strong landing force embarked in the boats and started for the landing. It was 6:30 A.M. The landing was made without resistance.

After about two hours the work ashore was completed. The landing force was making ready to re-embark when the *Emden* sent a signal by searchlight, "Expedite work!" Shortly thereafter the *Emden* blew her siren. That meant danger. The landing force saw the *Emden* quickly hoist her anchor, turn around and leave the harbor. The attempt to cut across the reefs and thereby catch up with the ship failed. Then in a few minutes *Emden* hoisted her battleflags and opened fire on an opponent that could not be seen from the boats. His presence, however, was denoted by the high splashes caused by shells striking close aboard the *Emden*.

Unable to be of the slightest assistance to their ship, the landing force was obliged to remain ashore gnashing their teeth and watching the unequal fight that was now in progress.

The *Emden*'s *vis-à-vis* was the English-Australian cruiser *Sydney*. She being one and a half times larger, five years younger, equipped with side-armor, and carrying a battery with the same number of guns per broadside as the *Emden*, but each gun one and a half times larger, and having the superior speed, the result of this engagement was never in doubt. The inevitable and fatal hour had struck.

Soon the ships engaged in a running fight at a range of about four to five thousand meters. Broadsides of "iron-greetings" were exchanged. At first it seemed as if the enemy had suffered heavily. The *Emden*'s salvos from the very beginning landed in the forward part of the enemy's ship. The gunnery of the English was not of a very superior order. Although our ship had been under fire for a considerable time, not one hit had been made on her. Then a heavy salvo landed on the *Emden*'s stern. The heavy shells easily penetrated the unarmored sides of the *Emden*, causing extraordinary damage. Fire broke out under the poop. For about 15 minutes flames shot 20 to 25 meters in the air out of the after end of the ship. The gray clouds were streaked with white steam, indicating that a steam pipe on the starboard side must have been pierced. These serious injuries did not, however, prevent the *Emden* from continuing her energetic attack on the enemy. She turned with full rudder and went after him.

The stream of projectiles from her bow guns never ceased. A few minutes after the *Emden* turned toward him the enemy cruiser also turned away to starboard and drew away from our ship. As we had meanwhile noticed that he had been hit several times, we, on shore, silently hoped that he had received some fatal injuries. Evidently this was not the case. He headed away at full speed, but shortly after he came about again. No doubt he was trying to increase the range in order to use his more powerful guns and still keep outside the effective range of the *Emden*'s lighter battery.

Meanwhile the *Emden* received some more serious injuries. While turning toward the enemy, a shell knocked the forward smoke-pipe down. This huge, bulky mass lay athwart the fore-castle. Almost at the same time another shell carried the fore-mast by the board. When I saw this I knew that at least one of my comrades lived no more—the control officer in the foretop.

The fire aboard the *Emden* continued to rage, seeming grad-ually to suffocate them all. Instead of flames we now saw clouds of smoke evidently caused by their attempting to put the fire out. Running along side by side, firing heavily all the time, the two engaged cruisers disappeared over the horizon.

The fight started shortly after 8.30 A.M. The *Emden*'s land-ing force now had to prepare an old schooner lying in the harbor, *Ayesha* by name, for a trip to sea in order to be able to leave the island in case the *Emden* did not return. As the day wore on we could, on several occasions, see the *Emden* near the horizon, but not near enough to be able to make out anything. Unfortunately, we could see from time to time large, black smoke-clouds, caused by the Indian or Australian coal which the *Sydney* was using. The landing force, therefore, had to assume that the fight was still going on.

Shortly before dark that evening both vessels again ap-proached. They still continued to fire. The last of the fight that the landing force saw was shortly before sunset. The *Em-den* was then steering at slow speed to the eastward. The ship was almost entirely under the horizon. Only one smoke-pipe and the mainmast remained standing, but they gave us the indications in regard to her course and speed.

The limit of visibility, that is, the distance from Keeling to the horizon, was about eight to ten sea miles. It was, therefore, certain that shortly before sunset the *Emden* not only remained afloat, but was not more than eight to ten sea miles distant from South Keeling. The *Sydney* was nearer the island. We could see her masts, smoke-pipes, superstructure and up-per deck. Both vessels still fired, but the *Emden*'s fire was intermittent and not very heavy. Either her ammunition was exhausted, for she had expended a considerable amount during the Madras bombardment and the Penang battle, or a majority of her guns were put out of action.

At sunset the *Sydney* broke off the engagement and steered in a northwesterly direction. *Emden* was heading easterly.

Gradually the ships drew outside of the range of their guns. The firing ceased.

The sun sets. It is getting dark. Like a shroud, night draws over both ships.

The landing force leaves Keeling on the *Ayesha* in order to hunt the *Emden*.

And so it happened that a ship, completely overpowered by the enemy, managed to continue the fighting for about ten hours. The combined advantages of armor, speed and armament need not be explained to those who are acquainted with naval affairs. On land, a small detachment, properly equipped, can utilize the natural surroundings to lie under cover behind wire defences with decked-over field-pieces and machine guns, and withstand a decidedly more powerful attacking foe for long periods, and even prevent his attaining his goal, as, for instance, an attempt to break through his line. The attacker cannot gain any decided advantage because of his superior numbers. His superiority is offset by the uses to which nature is put by the weaker defending force.

But at sea it is very different. There is no protection. The result is invariably decided in favor of the personnel enjoying the superiority of gunfire, the greater thickness of armor, and the superior speed.

Considering these factors, it becomes very evident that the *Emden* fought against heavy odds. Unarmored, decidedly smaller, handicapped by an inferior battery and slower speed than her armored opponent, she still managed to battle for half a day until darkness put an end to the engagement.

During the night the landing-force failed to pick up the *Emden*. Not until three weeks later, on their arrival at Penang, did they learn of the fate of their ship.

The song is ended. *Emden* is no more. The rocky reefs of North Keeling became her grave.

But just as long as the monsoons whisper through the high-crowned palms of this now world-famous island, joining the white, foaming surf of the Indian Ocean in singing the death song of the *Emden*, that long will people speak and sing of "The Flying Dutchman," the little German ship that, in the great World's War of 1914, cruised in great circles around in the open ocean, and, for months at a time, put the fear of God into the enemy.

> Schiff ohne Hafen, Schiff ohne Ruh,
> Fliegende, fliegende Emden Du.
> Deutscher Lorbeer um Mast und Bug,
> Hinter Dir her der englische Fluch.
> Schiff um Schiff in den Grund hinein
> Und das Meer, und das Meer, und das Meer war Dein.

> Schiff ohne Hafen, Schiff ohne Ruh,
> Herrliche, herrliche Emden Du.
> Wärst nun getroffen von feindlicher Hand?
> Wärst nun vergangen in lodernen Brand?
> Wärst nun versunken im weiten Meer?
> Wärst nun gestorben? Nein, nimmermehr, nimmermehr.

> Schiff ohne Hafen, Schiff ohne Ruh,
> Unvergessliche Emden Du.
> Kannst ja nicht sterben, es jagt daher
> Ewig Dein Schatten über das Meer.
> Ewig dem Feinde zu Fluch und Leid.
> Ewig in deutscher Unsterblichkeit.[1]

---

1. TRANSLATOR'S NOTE.—The foregoing is quoted verbatim in German so that the German reader may not lose the sentiment in these verses. The following translation is submitted with many apologies, etc., to the author.

Ship without harbor, ship without rest, / Our fleeing *Emden*, we love thee best. / Singing thy deeds in German verse, / Ever behind thee the English curse. / Ship after ship sent down to the deep, / But the sea, the broad sea, was thine to keep.

Press Clippings

[*Norddeutsche Allgemeine Zeitung*, November 12, 1914]
THE "EMDEN" AND HER COMPULSORY GUESTS

The adventures of four English captains whose vessels were sunk by the *Emden* in the Indian Ocean are reported in the *Ceylon Times* of September 29, 1914, as follows:

Captain J. J. Tullock of the *Tymerie* relates: We left Colombo on Friday (Sept. 25) and sailed along until at 11.25 P.M. we ran across a man-of-war without lights. The warship, which, as we later discovered, was the *Emden*, sent us a signal by lantern to stop. A boat, commanded by a lieutenant, was lowered and approached us. The officer said to me: "We are a German man-of-war and I want to see your ship's papers." Then they gave us 10 minutes to leave the ship and informed us that we were prisoners. After the Germans had searched the ship for provisions and the last boat had left our ship, we heard a muffled explosion. They had blown up the ship and she sank in the ocean. The chief engineer and I were taken aboard the *Emden* and treated very decently. They would not provide us with lights at night. But the officers gave us cards so that we could play during the day. The ship was full of living things, and even though they had many provisions which they took from captured ships, they seemed to be using them very sparingly."

Captain J. Isdale of the *Ribera* (sunk 300 miles west of Colombo) said: "My mate saw him first. 'Cruiser in sight, captain,' he called to me. Then the cruiser made the signal 'Stop immediately!' I said to the mate, 'Tell him, he has no

---

Ship without harbor, ship without rest, / Wonderful *Emden*, we love thee best. / Even though struck by the enemy shell, / Even though burned by a raging hell, / Even though sunk on a far away shore, / Hast been forgotten? No, nevermore.

Ship without harbor, ship without rest, / Memorable *Emden*, we love thee best. / Thou hast not died, ever we see / Thy flying shadow racing the sea. / Always the curse of the foe to be / Ever thy deeds in our memory.

right to stop us before he shows his flag.' The next instant the flag was hoisted. 'Damn we are finished!' Then an officer boarded us and said, 'Gather up as much clothes as possible and be quick about it, your ship is about to sink.' Then he asked about provisions and took everything along with him because, he said, they had to have them to live on. Otherwise he was very friendly. 'What would you, captain, 'tis the luck of war.' He gave me a half hour to take everything we wanted to the *Grypevale*, a captured ship, that was to take the prisoners to Colombo, the nearest English port."

Captain W. H. Gibson of the *Foyle* (sunk 315 miles off Colombo): "The German officers were very polite. I may say extraordinarily polite. Before we left in the *Grypevale* for Colombo, they all wished us a pleasant journey."

Captain D. Harris of the *King Lud*: " 'Unfortunately we have no harbor to which to send you; as you all did to our ships,' said the officer who came on board my ship. 'Get ready to leave your ship. She must be sunk within one hour.' "

[*Norddeutsche Allgemeine Zeitung*, November 8, 1914]
HOW THE "EMDEN" SHOT UP MADRAS

Brief news reports are now drifting in regarding the bold deed of our *Emden*, who, when she bombarded Madras, gave the Englishmen a wholesome scare.

"The night of September 22d was quiet and peaceful," says a reporter from Madras in describing the event. "The moon was not shining, and thick clouds hid the skies, when suddenly, about four kilometers outside of the harbor, there appeared an unusual light. A series of detonations followed, suggesting heavy explosions. Several seconds later the grayish, white light was replaced by high red flames that illuminated the whole sky, accompanied by powerful crashes and booming, and then all was still. I ran from my veranda to the roof of my house where the rolling flames could be seen much more easily and where I could hear many other noises such as the rattling of autos, tooting of trumpets, and the ringing of bells in the new court house. What had happened? We had known for several days that the German cruiser *Emden* was in the Bay of Bengal. She had captured and sunk several ships in the northern part of the bay and it was rumored that she would probably eventually visit Madras. Evidently that is what had happened. The cruiser had quietly approached until she was a short distance from the harbor and, from there, she sent her messengers of destruction into the city. One projectile fell in the bed room of the director of the Burmah Oil Company. He ran down stairs in order to get his wife and family to safety, when he saw a shell hit on the petroleum tanks; a few minutes later a shell set fire to one of the other tanks. Giant flames burst forth. One of the men on night watch was killed, another wounded. Also an Indian policeman was killed down in the harbor; his body was found later on in the water. One shell fell on a ship in the harbor, killing and wounding several people. As soon as the oil tanks caught fire, the *Emden* fired a few more shots into the town that fell in various different localities. The defences of Madras are not very strong, but there are several guns here that now came into action. After the third shot from these guns, *Emden* put out her searchlights, which were in use during the bombardment, and disappeared into the darkness. Unfortunately, Madras has no searchlights with which she might have been picked up."

In another letter concerning the bombardment, an officer from Madras writes: "The captain of the *Emden* is a Sahib [gentleman]. He wanted to do some damage to the town, but to spare as many lives as possible. He had officers and men aboard who knew Madras perfectly. The ships in the harbor were easier prey than the petroleum tanks. Why did he not shoot at the ships? He knew that if he managed to set fire to the oil tanks the burning oil would flow into the harbor and set fire to the ships. For this reason I say that the *Emden*'s captain is a Sahib. But his shells struck empty tanks and those that contained refined illuminating oil. So he did not quite succeed in his task."

Brief Descriptions of *Emden* and *Sydney*

"Emden"

Built at Danzig. Commissioned, Fall of 1908.

Authorized, 1906. Laid down, June, 1906. Launched, May 26, 1908.

Length, 386.6 feet. Beam, 44.3 feet. Draught (mean), 15.8 feet.

Displacement, 3592 tons.

I. H. P., 16,168, equals 24.1 knots.

Coal capacity, 393 to 836 tons.

Engines, two sets triple expansion reciprocating.

Boilers, 12 Schultz.

Armor, deck, 2 inches to .8 inch. Conning tower, 3.9 inches.

Armament, 10 4.1-inch (40 caliber); 2 machine guns. Torpedo tubes, 2 18-inch submerged on broadside.

Complement, 361.

"Sydney"

Built at Govan.

Laid down, April 14, 1911. Launched, May 30, 1912.

Length, 456.5 feet. Beam, 49.8 feet. Draught (mean), 15.7 feet.

Displacement, 5400 tons.

I. H. P., 22,000, equals 24.7 knots.

Fuel capacity, coal, 650 to 1000 tons; fuel oil, 250 tons.

Engines, 4 shafts, Parsons turbines. Boilers, Yarrow.

Armor, belt, 3 inches; deck, 1 inch.

Armament, 8 6-inch (50 caliber); 4 3-pdr.; 4 machine guns. Torpedo tubes, 2 21-inch submerged on broadside.

Complement, 376.

The *Emden-Sydney* Engagement

Extracts from a letter written by an English naval officer aboard H.M.S. *Sydney*, describing this engagement, taken from the *London Times* of December 15, 1914.

"On November 9 we were steaming about 50 miles to the eastward of the Cocos Islands (southwest of Java), heading for Colombo, when at 7 A.M. we took in a very interrupted wireless message from the Cocos wireless station: 'Strange warship. . . . off entrance.' The *Melbourne*, as senior officer, ordered us to raise steam for full speed and go and investigate.

"At 9.15 A.M. the tops of the cocoanut trees of Keeling Islands were sighted. At 9.20 we sighted the *Emden*, or rather the tops of her funnels, 12 or 15 miles away. At 9.40 A.M. she opened fire at a very big range, and shortly after that we started in on her.

"Throughout the action I was almost constantly engaged running backwards and forwards between the ammunition hoist and the forecastle gun or between the hoist and No. 1 starboard or No. 1 port.

"The hottest part of the action for us was the first half-hour. We opened fire from our port guns to begin with. I was standing just behind No. 1 port, and the gunlayer (Atkins, 1st class petty officer) said, 'Shall I load, Sir?' I was surprised, but deadly keen there should be no 'flap,' so said, 'No, don't load till you get the order.' Next he said, '*Emden*'s fired, Sir.' So I said, 'All right, load, but don't bring the gun to the ready.' I found out afterwards that the order to load had been received by the other guns 10 minutes, and my anti-'flap' precautions, though they did not the slightest harm, were thrown away on Atkins, who was as cool as a cucumber throughout the action.

"Later I heard a crash and looking aft saw that a shell had hit near Gun No. 2 starboard. But owing to the screen being in the way, I did not know it had knocked out practically the whole of that gun's crew. Not seeing any flame or smoke rising, (we cope with the smallest fire immediately) I went on with my job. This required continual attention. The men are splendid at loading drill, but to practise supply of ammunition is almost impossible in peace time. To have a big supply stacked on the upper deck is far too dangerous a proceeding

in action, and what with getting an even distribution of projectiles and cartridges between the two guns, getting the
safety caps off, with fiddly pins and things to take out, attending to misfires, cheering up the one or two who seemed
to be 'pulling dry,' you can imagine I had little time to be
thinking much about the *Emden*. I noticed once or twice when
going forward the starboard side to the forecastle gun that we
seemed to be in the thick of it. There was a lot of 'Wheee-
oo, Wheee-oo, Wheee-oo,' and the 'But-but-but' of the shell
striking the water beyond, and as the range was pretty big,
this is quite possible, since the angle of descent would be
pretty steep.

"Coming aft, I heard a shot graze the top of the shield of
No. 1 starboard. A petty officer now came up limping from
aft, and said that he had just carried an officer below (he was
not dangerously hit), and that the after control position had
been knocked right out and every one wounded (they were
marvelously lucky). I told him if he was really able to carry
on to go aft to No. 2 starboard and see there was no fire, and
if there was that any charges about were to be thrown overboard at once. He was very game and limped away aft. He
got aft to find a very bad cordite fire just starting. He with
others got this put out. I later noticed some smoke rising aft,
and ran aft to find that it was just the remains of what they
had put out, but found two men, one with a badly wounded
foot, sitting on the gun platform, and a petty officer lying on
the deck a little further aft, with a nasty wound in his back.
I found one of the men was unwounded, but badly shaken.
However, he pulled himself together when I spoke to him,
and told him I wanted him to do what he could for the
wounded. I then ran back to my group.

"All the time we were going 25 and sometimes as much
as 26 knots. We had the speed on the *Emden* and fought as
suited ourselves. We next changed round to starboard guns
and I then found the gunlayer of No. 1 starboard had been
knocked out close to the conning tower, so I brought Atkins

over to fire No. 1 starboard. I was quite deaf by now, as in the hurry there had been no thought of getting cotton wool. This is a point I won't overlook next time.

"Coming aft the port side from the forecastle gun I was met by a lot of men cheering and waving their caps. I said, 'What's happened?' 'She's gone, Sir, she's gone.' I ran to the ship's side, and no sign of a ship could I see. If one could have seen a dark cloud of smoke, it would have been different. But I could see no sign of anything. So called out, 'All hands turn out the lifeboats, there will be men in the water.' They were just starting to do this when someone called out, 'She's still firing, Sir,' and every one ran back to the guns. What had happened was a cloud of yellow or very light colored smoke had obscured her from view, so that looking in her direction one's impression was that she had totally disappeared. Later we turned again and engaged her on the other broadside.

"By now her three funnels and her foremast had been shot away, and she was on fire aft. We turned again, and after giving her a salvo or two with the starboard guns saw her run ashore on North Keeling Island. So at 11.20 A.M. we ceased firing, the action having lasted one hour and 40 minutes.

"Our hits were not very serious. We were 'hulled' in about three places. The shell that exploded in the boys' mess deck, apart from ruining the poor little beggars' clothes, provided a magnificent stock of trophies. For two or three days they kept finding fresh pieces. The only important damage was the after control platform, which is one mass of gaping holes and tangled iron, and the foremost range-finder shot away. Other hits, though 'interesting,' 'don't signify.'

"We started chasing a collier which had been in attendance on the *Emden*, and when we boarded we found they had opened the sea cocks and the ship was sinking fast, so we took every one off her and returned to the *Emden*, getting back there at about 4 P.M.

"They sent a man aloft to cut down the colors, and waved

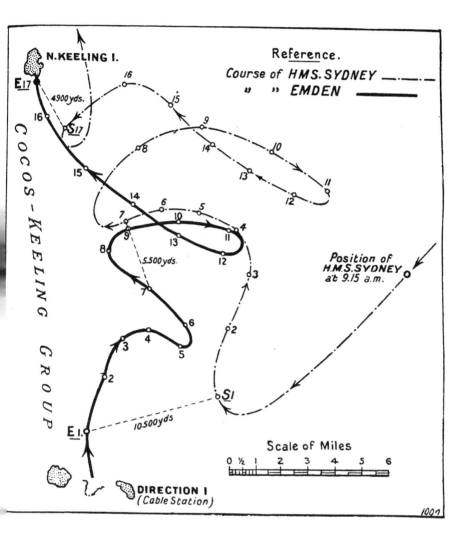

a big white flag from forward. It was getting dark and we
did not know for certain that the cruiser *Königsberg* might not
be near, so we could do no rescue work that night and had
to steam away. A cry in the darkness, and we stopped, and
lifeboats were lowered to pick up a nearly exhausted, but very

lucky German sailor. The fourth rescued from the water that day.

"November 10.—Early in the morning we made for the cable station, to find that the party landed by the Germans to destroy the station had seized a schooner and departed. The poor devils aren't likely to go far with a leaking ship and the leathers removed from all the pumps. Although they had broken up all the instruments, the cable people had a duplicate set buried, so that was satisfactory.

"At 11.10 A.M. we arrived off the *Emden* again. I was sent over to her in one of the cutters. Luckily her stern was sticking out beyond where the surf broke, so that with a rope from the stern of the ship one could ride close under one quarter, with the boat's bow to seaward. The rollers were very big, and the surging to and fro and so on made getting aboard fairly difficult. However, the Germans standing aft gave me a hand up, and I was received by the captain of the *Emden*. I told him from our captain that if he would give his parole the captain was prepared to take all his crew on board the *Sydney* and take them straight up to Colombo. He stuck a little over the word 'parole,' but readily agreed when I explained the exact scope of it. And now came the dreadful job of getting the badly wounded into the boats. There were 15 of these. Luckily we have a very good pattern of light stretcher into which men can be strapped. We got three badly wounded in each boat. The Germans were all suffering badly from thirst, so we hauled the boats' water casks up on deck, and they eagerly broached them, giving the wounded some first.

"I took an early opportunity of saluting the captain of the *Emden* and saying, 'You fought very well, sir.' He seemed taken aback, and said 'No.' I went away, but presently he came up to me and said, 'Thank you very much for saying that, but I was not satisfied. We should have done better. You were very lucky in shooting away all my voice-pipes at the beginning.'

"When I got a chance, with all the boats away, I went to

have a look round the ship. I have no intention of describing what I saw. With the exception of the forecastle, which is hardly touched from fore-bridge to stern post, she is nothing but a shambles, and the whole thing was most shocking. The German doctor asked me to signal for some morphia, sent me aft, and I never came forward again.

"Of the German officers, Witthoef, the torpedo lieutenant, was a thoroughly nice fellow. Lieutenant Schal was also a good fellow, and half English. It quite shook them when they found out that the captain had asked that there be no cheering on entering Colombo, but we certainly did not want cheering with rows of badly wounded men laid out in cots on the quarter deck. Captain von Muller is a very fine fellow.

"At Colombo we dropped all our wounded cargo, English and German. From the number of men we rescued, *i.e.,* 150, we have been able to reckon their losses. We know the number of men who landed at Cocos and got away, and the number of the prize crew in the collier. They cannot have lost less than 180 men killed, with 20 men badly wounded and about the same number slightly.

"There are lots of redeeming points in the whole show. Best of all was to see the gun's crew fighting their guns quite unconcerned. When we were last in Sydney we took on board three boys from the training ship *Tingira,* who had volunteered. The captain said, 'I don't really want them, but as they are keen I'll take them.' Now the action was only a week or two afterwards, but the two of the three who were directly under my notice were perfectly splendid. One little slip of a boy did not turn a hair, and worked splendidly. The other boy, a very sturdy youngster, carried projectiles from the hoist to his gun throughout the action without so much as thinking of cover. I do think for two boys absolutely new to their work they were splendid.

"It was very interesting talking to some of the German officers afterwards. On the first day they were on board one said to me, 'You fire on the white flag.' I at once took the matter up, and the torpedo lieutenant and an engineer both said emphatically, 'No, that is not so, you did not fire on the white flag.' But we did not leave it at that. One of us went to the captain, and he got from Captain von Muller an assurance that we had done nothing of the kind, and that he intended to assemble his officers and tell them so.

"The day Captain von Muller was leaving the ship at Colombo, he came up to me on the quarter deck wounded, shook hands and saluted, which was very nice and polite of him. I think, acting under their rules, he and his crew refused to give parole after their arrival at Colombo, but he conscientiously observed it while in the *Sydney,* which was more like a hospital ship than a man-of-war, while running to Colombo. Prince Hohenzollern was a decent enough fellow. In fact, we seemed to agree that it was our job to knock one another out, but there was no malice in it."

CHAPTER 8

Keeling Islands

"I RESPECTFULLY REPORT THE landing force, consisting of 3 officers, 6 petty officers and 40 men, ready to leave the ship."

It was at 6.30 A.M., on Nov. 9, 1914, that I made this report on the bridge to Commander von Mueller, commanding H.M.S. *Emden*. She lay at anchor at Port Refuge, which is the harbor built among the reefs of Keeling. Before long the two cutters contained the officers and men of the landing force. The steam launch was ready to take them in tow. The instructions that I received from the captain were to destroy the radio and cable stations on Direction Island (the most northerly of the Keeling group), and, if possible, capture and bring aboard all signal books, secret codes and other similar books.

From Direction Island there extend three cables: one to Mauretius, one to Perth in Australia, and the third to Batavia. As this station was the last link in the only straightaway cable from the home country (England) to Australia—the other cables having been previously destroyed by the other cruisers— it was reasonably certain that some attack could be expected there. Therefore, all four machine guns of the *Emden* were taken along. Two were in the steam launch, while each of the two cutters carried one. The men were armed with rifles, side-arms and revolvers. The steamer took the cutters in tow and we were off toward Direction Island.

Even small craft must navigate the inner atoll channels very cautiously in order to avoid the countless coral reefs that are promiscuously scattered about. The course that we laid off from the ship to the landing place was approximately 3000 meters long.

Direction Island is a flat plane with high palms. Among the tops of the palms could be seen the roofs of the European houses and the wireless masts. We set our course for these. Close in toward the landing lay a small white sailing ship at anchor.

"Shall we blow her up, too?" asked my lieutenant, nodding toward the sailer.

"Certainly," said I. "She has made her last trip. Detail a man at once to get the bombs ready."

With machine guns ready for action and small arms at hand, we landed, without resistance, at a small dock and immediately took up the march toward the radio masts.

The blowing up of the white ship was postponed, because I wished to see first what preparations had been made ashore.

Quickly we captured the telegraph station building and the radio station, preventing the further sending of signals. Then I ordered an Englishman, who was following us about, to call the director. He appeared shortly. He was a very easy going and prosperous looking gentleman.

"I have orders to destroy the cable and radio stations. I warn you therefore not to resist. Above all, it is to your interest to surrender the keys to the various buildings in order to relieve me of the necessity of breaking down the doors. Deliver all the weapons in your possession. Likewise have all Europeans gather in the open square in front of the telegraph building."

The director seemed to take these orders quite peacefully. He had not thought of resisting, he said, and, reaching down in his pocket, drew forth the keys and pointed out the houses in which were kept the remaining apparatus and then left, saying, "I congratulate you."

"Hm—what for?" was my apparently eager question.

"The Iron Cross. The Reuter telegram has been sent."

We then busied ourselves with bringing down the wireless mast. The torpedo-gunners brought their explosives and first the guys were parted, and finally the mast itself was brought to earth and chopped into short lengths.

In the telegraph office, the Morse keys were still working. We could not read what they were sending as it was in secret code, but it amused us to see the astonished faces of the operators when they received no answers to their signals because from the operation of the signal apparatus we could see that the senders were urgently calling for confirmation and acknowledgment.

The next job was a joy to the men. Without delay a pair of heavy axes were produced and in the next instant a shower of Morse keys, ink-wells, table legs, severed cable ends and similar wreckage flew about the room. They certainly obeyed orders to do a most thorough job. High and low, search was made for reserve instruments and such, and everything which appeared to belong to the station was destroyed. Among other things, a seismograph that had been installed on the island was also wrecked. Our men thought that it was a part of the telegraphic apparatus.

The heaviest work was the hunting for and cutting of the submerged cables. A chart containing the position of the cables could not be found in the stations, but along the beach were several signs marked "Cables." Here must be the land-end of the cables. With the steam launch we searched with a pair of drags or grapnels that are ordinarily used in fishing for cables. The work was not easy as we had nothing but manpower to use and that in very cramped quarters and the cables were exceedingly heavy. It was impossible to lift them to the surface of the water, so my men, after the bight of the cable had been raised a bit, had to dive and secure tackles to them so that we could proceed with the work. After much labor we were finally able to raise the cable strands up to the boats. I was unwilling to use explosive bombs with which to cut the cables as the *Emden* needed these to sink more merchant ships. We therefore had to cut the thick cables with crowbars, axes, chisels and other similar tools. After soul-wrecking efforts we succeeded in severing two cables and towing the dead ends to sea with the steamer. The third cable, in spite of an especially thorough search, was still undiscovered.

A small, corrugated-iron house containing a mass of reserve parts and all sorts of reserve apparatus was blown up by a bomb and burned down, while the newspapers, books, Morse messages and so forth, were taken along.

The landing party was getting ready to re-embark when the *Emden* signaled, "Expedite work." Thereupon I gathered up my men, gave up the destruction of the schooner lying in the harbor and was about to shove off when it was reported to me, "*Emden* blew her siren." According to orders this was to be the signal for returning aboard with the greatest despatch. As I got into the steamer I saw the *Emden*'s anchor flag at half-mast which meant that she was weighing anchor. The harbor was strange, but that made no difference to me. I was striving to return aboard as soon as possible. At full power I raced to the ship by the shortest route regardless of the reefs. The *Emden* in the meantime headed to sea at high speed. My first thoughts were that she was going out to intercept our tender *Buresk* (that had been ordered there to coal the *Emden*) and pilot her in through the reefs, and for that reason I continued to follow the *Emden* out, but was most astonished to discover that she was going at 16 or 17 knots. The steamer, with two heavily laden cutters in tow, could not exceed 4 knots.

Shortly the *Emden* hoisted her battle-flags and the starboard broadside opened fire. Even then I did not guess what it meant and thought perhaps that the *Emden* was trying to capture a steamer which she had discovered in that vicinity.

Then a salvo of five heavy shells fell behind the *Emden*, and the five large splashes indicated the source of the firing. Now we knew that a real, earnest engagement was going on. The enemy we could not see. He was still hidden by the island and its palms. *Emden* had by now steamed several thousand meters away and was increasing the distance between us very rapidly so that I gave up all hopes of joining her. Therefore I came about.

CHAPTER 9

Ayesha

W E RETURNED TO THE SAME landing. I gathered the Englishmen together again, took away all their firearms, hoisted the German flag over the island, according to the rights of war, forbade any attempts at communication by signals with the other islands or with enemy ships, and gave orders to my officers to prepare the beach for defense, to mount the machine guns and to stand by to dig trenches. I reasoned that the engagement of the ships would be a short one and that I would certainly have to reckon with the enemy ship which would return to inspect the station. Nevertheless I had no idea of surrendering the island, over which flew the German flag, without a struggle.

The Englishmen, slightly disturbed, came and asked permission to withdraw to another part of the island in case a fight became imminent. To which I agreed.

With two signal-boys, I withdrew to the roof of the largest house in order to observe the fight. The English were, all in all, not much concerned over the engagement of the cruisers several thousand meters from the island. They seemed to confine their interests to other things. One of them approached one of the officers who was at work on the beach and laughingly, in a friendly tone, asked "Do you play tennis?"

A question which, under prevailing conditions, seemed to us most inconceivable.

When I reached the roof, the fight between the *Emden* and the other cruiser was at its height. Both vessels were firing heavily with each broadside. I did not know the name of the enemy ship, except that due to her construction and the aforementioned salvos, I judged her to be one of the Australian cruisers *Sydney* or *Melbourne*. I thought that the enemy must be armed with 15-cm. guns because the splashes were higher and larger than those which the *Emden*'s shells would make.

The *Sydney*, as I later discovered her to be, was much more heavily armed than the *Emden*. Our ship, of 3600 tons, could bring to bear five 10.5-cm. guns to a broadside, and she had no side armor. On the other hand, the *Sydney*, of 5700 tons, could bring five 15.2-cm. guns to bear on the broadside, and she had side armor. As seen on a line, the *Emden*'s salvos seemed to be landing safely on the enemy cruiser, who was evidently firing very poorly, his shells landing several hundred meters apart. When he, however, succeeded in landing a salvo, the destruction on an unarmored ship was very severe.

At the very beginning of the fight the forward smokepipe of the *Emden* was brought down and lay across the ship. Another salvo, landing under the after cabin, started a fierce fire; gray clouds, caused by the lighter steam clouds mingling with the smoke, indicating that some steam-pipe must have been pierced.

Emden immediately turned short on the enemy and headed toward him at full speed, evidently with the intention of attacking him with torpedoes. While doing this her foremast went overboard. For an instant it seemed as if her adversary wished to break off the engagement as he steamed away at top speed, followed by *Emden*. Whether he had received any severe injuries, not apparent from outside the ship, I could not make out. Perhaps also he was endeavoring to increase the range so that his superior armament could be used to better advantage. The fight drew toward the northward away from the island until finally both vessels, still fighting, were lost below the horizon.

The question now arose as to what disposition I should make of the landing force. Our ship had already received such severe punishment by the more powerful ship that it was next to impossible for her to emerge victorious and return to the island. She would probably have to arrange to slip into some harbor in order to make repairs, bury the dead and transport the wounded ashore. I could, however, safely assume that in a short time some English warship would proceed to Keeling to see what was happening to the radio and cable stations. The telegraphic communications were broken between the Australian ports and also between Batavia and Mauretius.

We could, with our 4 machine guns and 29 rifles, repulse a landing force of Englishmen, but we were powerless against the gunfire which the English cruiser would pour on us. All in all, it seemed but a postponement of the inevitable surrender of a post whose loss was, without doubt, a foregone conclusion. Captivity in English hands was not to our taste.

There still lay in the harbor the small, white schooner, fortunately not as yet blown up. It could and would help us out. I decided to leave the island on it. The name was *Ayesha*[1] and it had formerly made two or three trips each year to Batavia, carrying copra away and returning with provisions. Now, however, as steamships made regular calls here, the schooner lay in the harbor unrigged, out of service and rotting away.

I went to her alone in the steam launch in order to look her over and determine her seaworthiness. The captain and one seaman were aboard. At first, in an offhand way, I asked

---

1. *Ayesha* is not an English but an Arabian name, and is pronounced (Ah) (ee) (shah). Ayesha is the name of the favorite wife of the prophet Mohammed.

him if he had any munitions aboard, as I did not wish him to guess the reason for my coming aboard. He denied having any, and while showing me casually about the ship, I concluded that she apparently was still seaworthy. Therefore I sent my officers and men to the *Ayesha* to prepare her for sea. And there was a lot to be done. All sails and rigging had been removed and stored and these had to be found and brought aboard.

As the English discovered my intention of leaving the island in the schooner, they warned me most carefully. The *Ayesha* was old and rotten and could not keep the sea. Also, they advised me that the English man-of-war *Minotaur* and a Japanese cruiser were near the island and that they thought that capture by them was certain. Also, my predecessor on the *Ayesha*, as he left the ship, said goodbye with the following words: "I wish you a *lucky* cruise, but the vessel's bottom is full of holes."

Inasmuch as we continued to prepare the *Ayesha* for sea, despite all their warnings, the English finally saw the sporting chance we were taking and then ran their legs off to assist us. I leave it to you to judge whether it was gratitude that drove them to be of assistance. Previously several of them had expressed their delight to me at the destruction of the cable service, as the many hours of extra work and the scarcity of reliefs were now at an end once and for all. They showed us where to find provisions and water, advising us to take provisions from this side only as they were new and fresh while those on the other side were old; they brought cooking utensils, water, casks of oil, old wearing apparel, bedclothes and similar most necessary stuff. Invitations to luncheon poured in from all sides. They gave pipes and tobacco to my men. In short, the English did everything they could to help us out. They did not deceive me in regard to courses and, as I later discovered, all their information in regard to wind, weather, currents, etc., was substantially correct. As the last boat left the beach they gave three cheers, wished us a pleasant voyage and thanked us profusely for the "moderation" which we employed in carrying out our task, in which all the people "generously" joined. Then they swarmed about the ship for a time taking photographs of the *Ayesha.*

In the meantime, the lookout reported that the two engaged ships were again in sight. From the *Ayesha*'s masthead I could see only the heavy, black smoke clouds of the *Sydney,* then the masts, smokepipes and superstructure gradually came in sight. On the *Emden* I could see only one smokepipe and one mast. The remainder of the ship was still under the horizon. Both cruisers were steering easterly courses. The firing was still going on.

Finally the *Sydney* shot out at high speed toward the *Emden.* I had the feeling that the *Emden* had made her last stand and that the *Sydney* was approaching to administer the final death blow. Then there showed between the foremast and the forward smoke-pipe in the black smoke of the Englishman a high, white water-spout that could only have been caused by a heavy explosion. We assumed it to be a hit by one of the *Emden*'s torpedoes. The *Sydney,* still at least 20 sea-miles away, turned hard to starboard and, on the opposite course, steered slowly to the westward, the *Emden* continuing on her easterly course. Both vessels still continued firing. The range became greater and greater until at last it exceeded the range of the guns. The engagement ceased, both ships disappearing beneath the horizon in the approaching darkness. That was the last I could observe. The fight started at about 8:30 A.M. and lasted until about 6 P.M. The story published in all the English newspapers that it was a "60-minute running fight" should be classed with the numerous other false English reports.

The coming of darkness then made it necessary for me to slip from the harbor. In the dark it is absolutely impossible to leave the harbor and navigate safely among the many coral reefs. We had in the meantime taken aboard enough water to last about four weeks and sufficient provisions for eight weeks.

The sails were, of course, made ready for use. I gave the crew a short talk, and then to the accompaniment of three cheers to the bravest of the war's heroes we hoisted the battle-flag and pennant on the latest acquisition to the navy, His Majesty's Ship *Ayesha*. The steam launch slowly towed us ahead. I took station in the foretop because, as we had no reliable charts, from there the reefs and channels could best be seen. With my battery whistle I gave orders to the towing steamer, telling them to avoid the reefs by steering to port or to starboard. The two *Emden* cutters I took in tow.

The trip out was very slow indeed for us. The sun was already setting and in the tropics there is no twilight. As soon as the sun disappears beneath the horizon, complete darkness reigns. We had not quite finished the dangerous passage among the reefs before it became too dark for me to make out the channel from my position on the foremast. Therefore I took station in the port chains close to the water's edge and directed the operations from there.

Just as we were passing the last reef which could possibly be dangerous, we received a bad scare. In spite of the darkness I could clearly see each stone, each blade of grass on the bottom, a sign that we were in shallow water. Our stern, however, went over the shoals without grounding.

In the interim we set several sail in order to lighten the heavy tow work of the launch. Soon we were clear of the protecting islands and, on the bosom of the ocean, our craft received a new motion, the heavy, long swell of the sea.

When we had proceeded sufficiently well out to be free to cruise without danger of the breakers, I recalled the steamer alongside in order to muster the crew. The high swells made this maneuver not an easy one. The steamer was constantly surging against the guard-rail of the *Ayesha*, and although I now seemed indifferent to the fate of the steamer, I still had many scruples against this unintentional duel between my new and my old ship. I doubted if the *Ayesha* could stand these friendly attentions very long, so it finally became expedient to cast off the steamer and the last man opened the throttle to use up the remaining steam in the boiler before he jumped aboard. With a boat-hook, we, on the *Ayesha*, put her rudder to port. In an elegant curve she drew away and was lost in the darkness. Where she wound up, I know not. Probably she found her grave in the breakers, roaring a few hundred meters away. Perhaps, also, she is still cruising on the ocean, carrying on a war of privateering.

The light cruiser *Emden*, often called "the Swan of the East." Built at the Imperial Shipyard at Danzig in 1906–9, she displaced 3,650 tons, carried a complement of 361 officers and men, and attained a trial speed of 25.1 knots. Her armament consisted of ten 10.5cm (4.1 inch) quick-firing guns and two 45cm (17.7 inch) torpedo tubes.

The Direction Island wireless and cable station staff posed beneath the Imperial German naval ensign with one of von Mücke's officers (*standing seventh from left*) and a guard, 9 November 1914.

The Germans dynamited the station's wireless mast but honored a British request to drop it clear of the tennis courts.

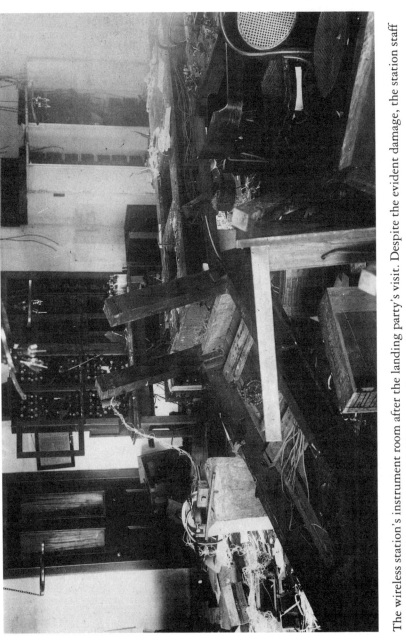

The wireless station's instrument room after the landing party's visit. Despite the evident damage, the station staff succeeded in making contact with Singapore that evening.

HMAS *Sydney*, the *Emden*'s nemesis. A considerably larger and more powerful light cruiser launched in 1912, she displaced 5,400 tons and was armed with eight 15.2cm (6 inch) guns and two 53.3cm (21 inch) torpedo tubes.

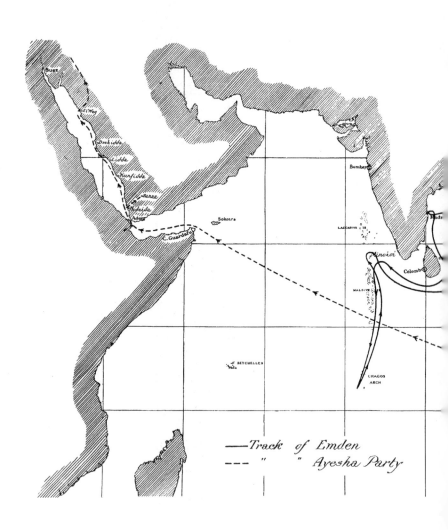

Track   of   Emden
---   "   " Ayesha Party

The landing party pushing off from Direction Island after hearing the *Emden*'s siren sound the recall. Von Mücke stands in the bow of the steam launch; his officers are seated, with sidearms, at the tiller of the cutters.

Hoping in vain to overtake the *Emden*, the landing party nears the anchored *Ayesha*.

The battered and burned-out *Emden* aground off North Keeling Island. Her wreck remained there until 1950, when a Japanese salvage company broke it up.

After returning to Direction Island, von Mücke's party removed provisions sufficient for a two months' voyage from the cable station's storehouse.

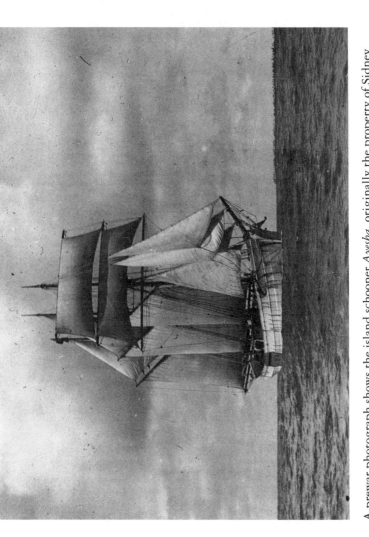

A prewar photograph shows the island schooner *Ayesha*, originally the property of Sidney Clunies-Ross, owner of the Cocos Keeling Islands, leaving for Batavia with a cargo of copra. "Ayesha" was the name of Mohammed's favorite daughter.

CHAPTER 10

On Board

THE NEXT DAY WE PROCEEDED to inspect more minutely our new home. The *Ayesha* was a ship of 97 tons gross, as we discovered by reading a sign on one of the beams in the storeroom. She was about 30 meters long and approximately 7 to 8 meters beam. The ship was fitted with three masts, the two after ones, that is, main and mizzen, were schooner-rigged, while the fore carried two square sails. Evidently she had been manned by a crew of five seamen and the captain, while we now had 50 aboard. The men were quartered in the crew's space forward. But as the forecastle could not accommodate more than six men, the remainder slept in the storeroom.

When we took her she had no cargo aboard, but she did have some iron ballast. It was not a pleasant job to fit out the crew for sleeping, as it had only been possible to bring along from Keeling a very small quantity of bedclothes and mattresses, and the men had to sleep on the spare canvas (sails) on top of the iron ballast. Step by step they gradually increased the comforts of their quarters. They speedily proceeded to make hammocks out of old ropes, binding twine, tattered scraps of sail and such material. These were then hung wherever there was room and thereby offered the possessors a refuge from the heavy rolling of the ship.

In the after storeroom were two small cabins under the deck which had been fitted out with sleeping accommodations, but were used by us as provision storerooms, as we could see that the innumerable cockroaches would make life unbearable. Way aft was still another small room which, from a sign over the door, we knew to be the navigation room. In this the petty officers quartered themselves.

On deck I found a small deck-house of two rooms, but only one bed. In one of these I lived; the other was shared by my two lieutenants. Finally, there was still another exceedingly small room that held a table and a couple of small benches. This we used as a messroom, as an office for the officer of the deck, as chart room, smoking room, lounging room, saloon, etc.

Several difficulties were found with the equipment on board. The canned provisions brought along from Keeling made very choice food, but the galley (that is, the ship's kitchen) was of course built to serve five men, and the dwarf stove therein was not of much use to us. Fresh water could not be used for cooking because it had to be conserved for drinking purposes only. We increased our capacity for cooking by tearing off promiscuously distributed pieces of sheet iron, laying them around the stove, and placing chunks of iron ballast, brought from the storeroom, on the sheet iron until we had a fire-proof foundation on which to start a fire. The men sat in circles holding their cooking utensils by the handles over the fire until the food was cooked. It was impossible to set a large pot over the fire because of the heavy rolling of the ship.

Cooking was done with salt water. The arrangements were placed entirely in the hands of the cook. The food aboard the *Ayesha* was not bad, consisting mainly of rice, fruit, ham, corned beef and such other provisions.

The question of drinking water was more important. There were four small, iron, fresh-water tanks aboard, constructed for the supply of the aforementioned crew of five men. When preparing the *Ayesha* for sea, we had no time to examine these carefully. We had to fill them as quickly as possible. Having used but from one tank, it was several days before we noticed that the other three tanks had become foul. The water was not drinkable. The assortment of Selters water that was brought from Keeling was to be used only as a last resort, because I had to plan to abandon ship in the two *Emden* cutters which I still carried, in case of accident to the *Ayesha*, of whose seagoing qualities I had not as yet been thoroughly convinced. In such a case the only way to carry water would be in the Selters bottles. We hoped at some future time to replenish our foul tanks with rain-water. And even this hope did not fail us. On the 13th of November, that is, four days out at sea, the first of the tropical rains came on. We had cleaned out our three bad tanks and rigged up an old sail as a rain sail. It was secured horizontally across the loading hatch. A hole was made in the middle of the sail and a man stood beneath the hole with a petroleum tin—that is, one of the containers in which the Standard Oil Company ships its petroleum—and caught the water as it dripped down through the hole in the sail. The full tins were then passed down the line of men to the tanks. In addition the cabin roof was also rigged to catch the rain. On the sides were small rails and the water which gradually filled the roof ran down two small drainpipes into the petroleum tins that we had hung up beneath them. The rain-water was drinkable, especially when we added a little lime juice (lime juice is a sour-tasting essence). We found a few flasks of it (lime juice) among the provisions of the former captain.

As the tropical rains came almost regularly morning and evening from now on, we soon had our tanks full of water. Also all possible water-bearing receptacles and petroleum tins were filled with water. In other directions the rain also came in handy. As the sweet water had, of necessity, to be saved for drinking purposes, we were in a bad way about washing. Soap will not make a lather in salt water, nor does salt water alone make one clean. We used the showers, therefore, to give ourselves a good sousing and washing. They became regular shower baths. We closed up the scuppers with old rags and such to prevent the water from flowing overboard. The water accumulated on deck, and washing from side to side as the ship rolled, together with the constantly falling clean water from above, gave us the finest baths imaginable.

The *Ayesha* carried two small boats. One held barely two men while the other, a larger one, not more than three men. They swung in davits abreast the cabin. These boats were also used to gather water in that the hole in the bottom was carefully closed by the plug. Even though the water, caught by this method, was not drinkable as we had hoped, due to the strong salty taste, it was not too salty to be sued for washing purposes.

The crew was divided into two watches, the starboard and the port watch. Most of my men had naturally seen service on a sailing ship and were familiar with the duties and rigging, but the firemen had never been in a position to be detailed to duties aboard sail craft. I had, however, so many erstwhile fishermen and sailing ship seamen in my complement that I could handle the ship in safety. When it became necessary to use all hands on deck in order to carry out any evolution, there was much strength available.

The rigging gave us our next great care. A large part of the sails were old and weak, ripping constantly, so that we were forever busy with patching and mending. Often the shrouds themselves carried away. Therefore we had to watch the weather signs very carefully as we had no idea how much of a blow the masts would stand. Considered as a ship the *Ayesha* inspired little confidence. The captain's words as he left the ship in Keeling, "The bottom is full of holes," seemed to be correct. In the storerooms, as we scratched the planking with a knife, we discovered how decayed and rotten the wood was, so we quickly desisted from scratching for fear of sticking the tip of the blade into the Indian Ocean.

The first day we had a following sea and the *Emden*'s cutters towing at the end of a long line did some wild dancing; while doing this one of the cutters rammed the overhanging stern of the ship and carried away the so-called mirror. (Note: The mirror is that part of the stern where the name or coat-of-arms is attached.) One of these scuffles between the boat and the ship itself resulted to the disadvantage of the former. The bow of the boat struck the rotten wood of the mirror a powerful blow and broke a plank just above the water line. I was not, however, disposed to chance a repetition of such a catastrophe, so I cast the ill-behaved cutter adrift and kept but one, which deported itself in a more gentlemanly way. But this precaution was not effective very long. I do not know whether it was, or was not, due to the example set by his brother whom I cast adrift, but in one of the next few nights he also disappeared, taking with him a piece of my rail to which he had been secured. The place where the rail carried away (evidently pulled out a cleat) showed how decayed and rotten the wood was.

In the first days the *Ayesha* filled up with water. In a very short time we had so much in the ship that it covered the iron ballast on which the men were sleeping. While endeavoring to work the ship's pump we discovered that it was broken. There was no piston packing. We took the pump apart, disconnected the pistons, and replaced the absent rubber packing with trouser rags soaked in fat, so that we could again start pumping out the ship. All in all the picture of the *Ayesha* classed as a seagoing ship was pretty sad. If we had had to receive a visitor at sea he would probably have been quite astounded at the paradise condition in which we were as regards clothing, for aside from the occasions on which the rainfall furnished us with baths, when we wore nothing at all, even at other times our clothing was quite scanty. Prior to landing at Keeling we dressed as lightly as possible, and I also directed that only the oldest clothes should be worn. Now, during the long continued sailing and due to the strenuous labor on board, the goods rapidly went to pieces. Means for bettering this condition were not at hand, as we had neither needles nor thread. True, we had brought along some old garments from the English at Keeling, but these served more as amusements than as regular clothing. I had the impression that the average Englishman was a tall and slender person. Whether that is true or not in Keeling I do not know, but these trousers came up to the calves of my men's legs, while the blouses and jackets were sufficiently large for any two men.

CHAPTER 11

A Fine Day Aboard

About 6 A.M., AT SUNRISE, the crew got up. Aboard men-of-war, reveille is usually sounded by seamen petty officers with pipes, so-called boatswain mates, who give three long, shrill whistles as a signal for all hands to turn out and lash hammocks. We tried the experiment of omitting this detail because we had but one boatswain's mate aboard and we could not count on his being on watch daily at this time. The men slept close together packed like sardines; it therefore became necessary to awaken only one man in order to get them all up, as he disturbed his neighbor who in turn passed the disturbance on from man to man.

After rising, each man washed up, utilizing the rain-water in one of the small boats, left over from the previous night. When times came when we could not wash we did not let that bother us; because our deportment otherwise harmonized with our condition, in that we of course had no tooth-brushes. Much attention was bestowed, however, on the hair which grew longer and longer. The single comb traveled from hand to hand, your neighbor acted as your mirror, and the water with which to wet your hair was very select salt water. For the "dandies" we even had a shaving kit, the rusty razor carving up their faces in all sorts of ways.

Then we turned to cleaning up the ship. With buckets we drew water from over the side and sprinkled the decks. One gang would turn to and pump out the water which had come in overnight. The old sailor men were examining the rigging to see what had again carried away, and then repaired it. The cook, with his chosen confidants, sat around the galley preparing breakfast. It usually consisted of rice with tea and coffee. Then there evidently seemed little more for the crew to do. Drills could not be held due to the lack of space. We sometimes passed the time away by instructing the staff-detailed men and the firemen in the secrets of steering, compasses, and the service, etc., of the rigging of a sailing ship. Frequently the men were shown the chart, the only one aboard, and the position of the ship explained to them. Plans were laid for the future.

Speaking of charts, we had, outside of the special chart of Batavia to which we would not go, one chart embracing half the world, made out on a ridiculously small scale. It reached from Hong Kong and Borneo in the East to Suez, Zanzibar and Mozambique in the West. The journey, some 700 sea-miles, to Padang where I wished to go, was, on this card, about as large as the breadth of your hand.

In the meantime it soon became noon and time for the noon meal. As we had not enough plates, forks, etc., to go around the crew had to eat by sections. The individual portions were dished out by the cook under the supervision of the petty officers. In addition to the food at noon, each man received a cup of coffee or tea. In order to break the monotony of a long afternoon, the meal was drawn out as long as possible and at its conclusion we took a nap. The separation of officers and men as practiced on large ships was here naturally wholly out of the question. The deck space was merely sufficient to permit all hands to lie down comfortably on the main deck.

Soon they formed groups that favored certain places to loaf.

There they sat or lay down, smoking or sleeping; or were considering themselves fortunate to be in line waiting for their turn to use one of the few decks of cards that we succeeded in digging up in Keeling. Others turned to fishing. All along the rail hung fishing lines lying in wait for the fish. To the best of my knowledge we did not catch a single one. Should that be blamed on the fact that fish do not bite on rice, our only bait? Many times were the old reminiscences retold, while picture puzzles, number tricks and foolish questions made their regular rounds.

In the evenings after supper, when the sun had set, the men would gather up forward and sing. As we had some good singers, the chords of the quartets were right musical, and, as usual when the Germans are in a good mood, "Loreley" and such other tragic songs are the favorites. In passing, I will not say that "Puppchen" (Doll) and "Das Lied von der Reeperbahn" (The Song of the Ropewalk) were forgotten.

We did not set a definite time for turning in. Each turned in when he pleased and the men on watch, that is, the lookout forward and the helmsman aft, saw to it themselves that they were properly relieved on time. We carried no lights at night. We had very little petroleum aboard, and the two petroleum lamps ready at hand made more smoke than light.

CHAPTER 12

A Restless Day

B UT NOT ALL DAYS passed by as comfortably as the one previously described. Frequently we battled with storms and rain squalls. Particularly was this true each morning and evening. Although the bad weather was pleasant in that it provided us with water, it nevertheless worried us because of the danger to ship and rigging. Luckily the storms and squalls can be seen, in the tropics, a long distance off and their approach can be clearly gauged.

On the horizon could be seen irregular, individual black clouds, and the rain could be seen as long and wide dark stripes. As the clouds floated higher, the rain would draw distinctly closer. When the storm approached within about a thousand meters, the sails were reefed as much as necessary and the storm ridden out. We lay this way close-reefed, only sufficient small sails set to keep her head into the wind, until the storm passed by, accompanied by such a heavy downpour that it was impossible to see anything but the closest objects.

One day we had a particularly heavy storm. The clouds flew so low that it almost seemed possible to reach up into them. The wind came up as we supposed, and, as we set to work to shorten sail, the squall struck us. It took the mizzen topsail and whipped it madly through the air a few times.

The men on deck could not hold on; the sail flew over the mizzen gaff, held fast there, and finally tore and remained hanging. Repairs were impossible, due to the heavy rolling of the ship. The whipping sail endangered the whole top, especially the top-mast, that is, the thin upper part of the mast, which is very poorly supported. It went through some hair-raising gyrations. It happened in the heaviest part of the squall when everybody had his hands full tending the other sails. Finally we managed to get in all sail except a few small rags that had to be set to keep headway or steerageway on the ship.

The clouds were so thick that it grew dark as night. Ear-splitting, shrill lightning flashes and heavy thunder followed. They were so near and so bright that they blinded one, making it impossible to see for a few seconds.

The heavy wind finally left the storm center and it became perfectly calm in the air. But the sea and swell kept running. When the masts lost the steady pressure of the wind she pitched about so wildly that we were afraid the masts would go by the board without our being able to do anything to prevent it. The air was charged with electricity, and St. Elmo's fire burned a foot high at each mast head.

Gradually the storm passed by. After several short but strong puffs of another squall, quiet weather set in and only the distant visible signs reminded us of the several bad hours we had recently passed through. Quickly we set all sail and proceeded. Soon thereafter a steady wind set in again.

At those times when there was absolutely no wind, the heavy swell of the high seas caused extraordinarily heavy pitching and rolling. The sails by now had very little support left, and as the yards and booms swung across the ship from side to side the masts and the whole ship trembled. On those occasions we were therefore forced to secure all sails and gear so as to prevent damage to the ship and its rigging.

Life on board was, therefore, because of the jerky motion, very uncomfortable and tiresome, for one had to stand holding on securely with both hands, or else wedge himself in some safe corner, in order to live. Also at these times we had to secure all sail.

One day while so disposed and while attempting to prevent our souls from jumping out of our bodies, a smoke cloud was reported on the port hand. As we were well off the beaten steamer tracks it could only mean that it was a ship likewise avoiding the regular steamer paths. Then we thought that it might be either the *Exford* or the *Buresk*, the colliers which the *Emden* had left at certain localities before the Keeling engagement, and that these colliers, not having heard further from the *Emden*, were also seeking to reach Padang and receive further information. Again, it might be some enemy cruiser which had been to Keeling, heard of our departure, and was now seeking us.

Now, when leaving Keeling, we had only three courses open to us: to Batavia, to Padang, or to Africa. The most evident (to the enemy) was either to Batavia or Padang. For a fast cruiser it would be an easy matter to search both tracks because he could, while we were delayed by weather, have laid down on the chart our probable courses and guessed at where we would most probably have arrived at a certain time.

All signs were investigated in endeavoring to determine the character of the ship. From the masthead we could see only the smoke. Any attempt to evade her with the *Ayesha* was impossible, as, without wind, we had no motive power. After several uncomfortable hours the smoke cloud disappeared.

Meantime the evening breezes came up, and with them the usual rain showers. To-day we received an unusual surprise. We found ourselves in the neighborhood where the southeast and northwest monsoons meet and fight for supremacy. Every instant the wind shifted. Soon a squall blew up from forward, and then came another from aft—a circumstance that called for the most delicate and special skill in the handling of the sails. We had practiced the shifting of sail several times before, but we were now given a job in which at first we had no idea what should be done. A heavy rain cloud from forward (to the northward) approached the ship simultaneously with one from aft (to the southward). Evidently we had to set the foresails for the storm from forward, and the sails aft in such a way as to ride out the storm approaching from the south. The two showers that accompanied the storms could not have been excelled by the shifting shower baths of the most modern sanatorium. The northern storm brought water that was so icy cold that the majority of us withdrew below deck; a moment later, the southern storm showered us with tepid, warm water.

CHAPTER 13

Padang

O N THE MORNING OF November 23, we "cleared" ship. We were approaching land and we decided that we were apt to find either a British or a Japanese destroyer coaling among the islands. In such case I had planned to cruise close to the unsuspecting destroyer and then, by an apparently unlucky accident, bring the ship alongside the destroyer and fire pointblank. Along the rail of the *Ayesha* we cut holes for our four guns so that we would have some sort of workable gun platforms for them and not be hindered by the miscellaneous tackle, hooks, etc. The rifles and revolvers were brought up on deck and the ammunition made ready. As the machine guns had not been used for some time we actually fired them as a trial.

About 10 o'clock in the morning, the lookout on the foremast sang out "Land ho." Owing to our defective navigational instruments we had no idea where we were and what land it was we had sighted. We were, however, pleased to be in the neighborhood of land. By and by, various islands came in sight. About 4 P.M. we had located ourselves as being off the

Sea-Flower Channel, about 80 miles from Padang. We had no chart of the Sea-Flower Channel, but we did know that numerous reefs were to be expected. As the evening calm had set in, and as I did not want to navigate the unknown channel at night, we came about, and under a few sail proceeded slowly to sea. Before sun up, we came about again and headed for the channel.

We stationed lookouts in the masts to watch for and report all changes of color in the water, as these are the forewarnings of shoals and reefs. With all sail set, a light wind carried us into the channel without encountering any extraordinary difficulties in navigation.

Now that we were certain that our water supply would hold out until we reached Padang, I gave each man a bottle of Selters water that probably tasted better now than it would have tasted previously. Shortly before 7 o'clock, our log registered the finish of the eight hundredth mile.

During the night a squall accompanied by a rain almost like a cloud burst gave us something to do. At daylight the next morning we could clearly see over the horizon the high mountains of Sumatra. Unfortunately the wind was off shore and very light, so that we hardly made any advance. Because of the intense heat at noon, we spread the awnings.

Our tobacco gave out entirely. The men smoked tea as a substitute. The officers also tried it. "Ye Gods, to ——." The crew however, seemed to enjoy it.

In order to navigate into Padang among the many islands and reefs, we used a chart which we found in an old seamanship book dug up in the ship, and while the chart was not a marvel for accuracy and detail, still we thought we were better off than if we had not found anything. In the evening we saw a lighted beacon on an island, the existence of which we had no previous knowledge. As the night wore on we finally recognized the distant glow of the lights of Padang. Unfortunately the current was setting us further away from land in-

stead of toward it and in the faint breeze it was impossible to
tack. The next morning found us five miles behind our position of the previous evening.

The straits, in which we now were, form the highway for
all ships. It was not very desirable for us to remain here very
long as we had to reckon on the enemy cruisers. As a dead
calm now ensued, we put both of our small boats in the water.
The one with one man, the other manned by two men, were
hitched up ahead of the *Ayesha*, and we endeavored by hook
or by crook to put some headway on her. The work of these
men, rowing in the glowing heat without any protection from
the sun, was not easy. But on board ship we did not idle. The
oars of the *Emden's* cutters that we had taken aboard before
abandoning the two cutters were brought on deck and lashed
together in pairs to increase their length. With these we attempted to row the *Ayesha* itself. Although we did not convert
her into an ocean greyhound, still we made some small headway.

Finally the following day a light wind sprang up that relieved us of the tedious work. In the distance, under the coast,
we could see numerous steamers that were either entering or
leaving Padang. One of these especially interested us as she
evidently had no destination, and as it was too deep to anchor
there, she must be lying to with her engines stopped. As we
approached her we could make out with certainty that she was
not a merchantship. She seemed to be a small man-o'-war, a
gunboat or a torpedo-boat destroyer. The ship carried a flag,
but due to the extreme distance we could not distinguish
which flag it was.

Soon we saw the apparently stopped ship get under way.
Heavy smoke clouds poured from her smoke-pipes, she turned
sharply toward us and approached at high speed. Shortly after
we recognized the Holland battle-flag. There was no object in
lifting our "incognito," and as we were in the open ocean
(outside the three-mile limit) there was no reason why we
should show our flag. We therefore hastily gathered our ar-

tillery and rifles together and stowed them below deck. All hands disappeared down the large hatch which was then covered over. The wildest looking sailor and I alone remained on deck. No one could guess that we belonged to the Imperial Navy because our naval uniforms were so very disreputable looking that we would sooner have been taken for members of the battle fleet of the South Sea Island states.

Soon the torpedo-boat destroyer arrived close aboard and displayed an uncommon, if not imprudent, interest in us. At a distance of 50 meters she passed by us at very slow speed. We saw the officers gathered together on the bridge armed with spy glasses and carefully noting all the details of our ship. From the lusty discussion among the officers we could see that they were talking about us. Close under our stern the destroyer came about and all eyes were riveted on the ship's name which long ago had been covered up by the thickest possible layers of heavy white paint. Slowly the destroyer proceeded ahead. We thought we had bluffed her out but, after she had steamed about 5000 meters away, she turned around and stopped. I could not overcome the feeling that she was waiting there for us.

As the destroyer approached us the battle-flag was already cleared for hoisting. Had she wanted anything from us we would have immediately hoisted our flag thereby presenting our visiting card.

In the course of the afternoon, our convoyer, whom we recognized by her name as being the Dutch destroyer *Lynx*, disappeared in the direction of Padang. Our original expectation that she had hurried on ahead in order to have the celebration prepared, the young ladies of honor ready and the triumphal arches erected, was not borne out by later events.

In the evening we were close in to the small low coral island guarding the entrance. The lights of an outcoming steamer could be seen from the harbor. Another was proceeding in towards the harbor. As we suspected that one of these craft must be our convoyer of the afternoon we carefully darkened the *Ayesha*. We were certain it was our old friend *Lynx* when the outcoming ship engaged in Morse signals with the entering ship. In spite of our precaution she unfortunately found us. She joined us and for some time her red and green lights could be seen close under our stern. She followed at a distance of about a hundred meters. We felt quite sorry for her for having to trundle along behind the *Ayesha*, which was proceeding at the high rate of scarcely one mile per hour—she could not make more in this light breeze. No doubt her machinists tending the 10,000 H.P. engines cursed us more than once. Her presence however was, from a navigational viewpoint, very desirable, because we now had no idea of our exact location, but where the *Lynx* could float, so could we also keep from grounding. We surmised that in case we approached a shoal, she would change course in plenty of time, and then we would follow her.

On the other hand, our convoyer would not pass ahead of us and we no doubt looked like a tramp being dragged home by a policeman. As we were a man-o'-war, we hadn't the slightest idea of allowing her to lead us along in this fashion. Therefore I tried to engage her in signal conversation and, to this end, had the white globe lantern, that usually hung in the crew's quarters, brought out. We held a board in front of the lantern, and by raising and lowering this lath we managed to make the Morse signs. By means of this most wonderfully perfected signal apparatus we finally managed to get the signal across, first in English, "Why do you follow me?" *Lynx* received the signal, made her acknowledgment, but did not answer. After about a half hour, having received no answer, we sent another Morse signal, but this time in German: "Warum folgen sie mich?" (why do you follow me?). This signal also was received. An answer did not come but shortly *Lynx* increased her speed and disappeared. The poor *Lynx* had to spend still another whole day in our neighborhood, as the wind failed again.

The next day, finding that the *Ayesha* had approached

within the limit of Holland's jurisdiction, I hoisted the battle-
flag and pennant. *Lynx* did not again approach any closer, but
always kept several thousand meters off.

About noon our situation became rather uncomfortable in
that we knew that we were in the region of reefs and even
we, with our very shallow draft, could not pass over them.
And we had no means of knowing the positions of the reefs.
Then a small Malay sailing boat came alongside carrying a
native pilot whom I employed. I had to promise him that the
German consul would pay him because the total wealth of the
entire ship amounted to one shilling two pence, that we found
in an abandoned purse of the previous captain, and which we
appropriated as war treasure for the Imperial Treasury. In con-
trast to the Dutch, as we later discovered, he seemed to make
a very favorable impression as a Malay pilot, as from the outset
he had no doubt as to our identity as a German man-o'-war
and declared himself to be perfectly satisfied to receive his pay
later on from the consul.

When the pilot boat came alongside, the *Lynx* shot over
toward us at the highest possible speed. As I knew not what
she wanted, I again hoisted the battle-flag which I had previously hauled down. And in order to create the impression
of equality, that the *Lynx* now found herself opposite an
Imperial man-o'-war, I ordered the crew to give the customary
honors between warships, as the *Lynx* shot by about 60 meters
away. The whole crew stood at attention on deck while the
officers saluted. Our greeting was returned by the *Lynx* in the
same manner.

Shortly before entering port I signalled the *Lynx*, "I will
send a boat." I jumped into my gala uniform, that is, my
khaki brown landing-force uniform used on *Emden*, that I had
saved for use against just such an emergency, and boarded her.

The captain met me at the gangway and ushered me into
the mess room. I opened the conversation. We were very
deeply affected by the intense interest which he had taken in
us for the last few days. We were the *Emden*'s landing force

that were now aboard H.M.S. *Ayesha*, en route to Padang, where we intended to repair the damages caused by the sea, and to look after our sea-going needs, consisting principally in filling up our provision and water supply. I asked if there were any objections to my ship entering the harbor. The captain answered that he had received orders to accompany us. There was no objection to entering port. We would, however, not be allowed to leave again. Above all, the rules to leave again would be laid down by the civil authorities ashore; he could give no definite assurances.

I contradicted him in that, as a man-o'-war, no one had the right to prevent our leaving again, adding laughingly, "I hope we two will not have an engagement when I leave again."

As I left the destroyer I saw for the first time, from a distance, the *Ayesha* under full sail. I must say that she made an excellent and pleasing impression, even though the pennant and battle-flag of the German Empire did not match the patched and torn sails.

On nearing the harbor, a small steamer brought the harbor-master aboard who was to show us where to anchor. He wanted to anchor us well out. It was my intention, nevertheless, to anchor close aboard the steamers lying in the harbor, which I could already see flew the German and the Austrian flags. Therefore I explained to him that I did not care to anchor way out, but that I would go further into the harbor. The ship would not be sufficiently protected out there, also I had not sufficient chain to anchor in the deep water. It was unnecessary to divulge to him that the chains could be used in water six times as deep. His original objections to my requests were gradually, by means of the German language, removed. By and by, as we were passing closer in and while he was energetically demanding that we immediately anchor, it so accidentally happened that both top sails, which were giving us a good deal of headway, could not be doused. Hacking away at the pin rail, etc., continued until, as I noticed, we were close to the steamers before it was possible to anchor.

As soon as the ship lay quietly at anchor, I sent my senior officer, Lieutenant Schmidt, ashore to the government officials to report my arrival and to explain my desires. At the same time. I invited the German consul aboard. I declared that I, in accordance with the customs of International Law, except by special agreement of the port authorities, must refuse any one permission to come aboard and also to refuse to allow any one to leave the ship.

Ayesha was immediately surrounded by great numbers of boats from the German ships. There were the Lloyd liners *Kleist, Rheinland* and *Choising*, and an Austrian. They also flew flags at their mastheads, and greeted us with a "Hurrah." They threw aboard cigars, cigarettes, tobacco, clocks, clothes, story-books, letters, and, most important of all, German newspapers. Of course they were old—they were up to October 2d, while this was November 27—still most welcome. As we had heretofore read only the English newspapers which we took from the steamers captured by the *Emden*, we knew nothing of the war except the villainous reports from Reuter, as, for example, Russians before Berlin, Kaiser wounded, Crown Prince killed, suicide epidemic among German generals, revolution in Germany, the last horse is being killed, complete defeat in the West, etc.

Along with the papers we also received pictures. As I returned to my room and to the mess room after a short absence, I found that the crew had nailed on the walls pictures of the Kaiser, a picture of the commander-in-chief of the high sea fleet, the Secretary of the Navy, and other such decorations.

The Dutch rules made a lot of trouble for me at first because they refused to acknowledge the ship as a man-o'-war and wanted to treat her as a prize. I therefore protested against the Dutch ruling and stated that it was my right as captain of this ship to acknowledge no superior authority except my accountability to Germany itself. Shortly thereafter I began to receive water, provisions, ropes, sail cloth, clothes, charts and the simpler requirements, such as soap, tooth-brushes, hairbrushes, boot-blacking, etc. The consul undertook to do the providing for us. One of the Dutch administrative officials, appointed "neutrality officer," got into communication with Batavia in order to consult as to how to apply the regulations. The impression that I received from everybody was unmistakable; they endeavored by every means to hold the *Ayesha* and intern the crew. It could plainly be seen that all the authorities were disturbed; fearing the anger of Japan or England, in case we left.

The principal man upon whom the decision rested seemed to be the harbor-master, a subordinate official, also a native Belgian. As the expected orders did not arrive by afternoon, I looked for the senior Dutch commander to inform him that no further orders had been received and that, according to the provisions of International Law, I had to leave again within 24 hours. About 7 o'clock a part of the expected orders had arrived. The neutrality officer brought them off. He took special pains to persuade me to intern my officers and crew. Having previously guessed this, I had both my officers take part in the conference so that he could learn at first hand the unanimity of the opinion of all officers.

Then he described to me such parts of the instructions from Batavia as he was permitted to divulge, the impossibility of getting away, he could not give us charts nor nautical books. Also many other things could not be obtained, such as "clothes." The delivery of these necessities was refused exactly like the delivery of soap, tooth-brushes, etc., that is, for the reason that they "increased our power."

We had not cleaned our teeth for over three weeks and now we had to wait a while longer. The single comb that had formerly served us all would have to continue doing so. As the harbormaster could see that my men had torn their clothes so badly that they were almost naked and because we had no charts, there seemed to be some special reason for the non-delivery of these most necessary articles. As I persisted that I would leave, charts or no charts, I was informed that I would certainly be captured, as the entire neighborhood was dotted with numerous Japanese and English cruisers. I had by luck managed to get in, but, on leaving, I would most certainly be captured. The *Emden* had done her work well and no one would think the worse of us if we gave up this undertaking which had no hope of success. It is understood, of course, that we refused all these previous proposals.

Meantime the provisions had arrived and we made ready to up-anchor. The 10 live pigs that we had taken aboard were in the way because they insisted upon standing where the anchor chain was being brought in. At 8 o'clock anchor was up.

We saw in the Dutch papers several weeks later that the people were concerned over the subject of what we were doing and where we were going. Had they paid attention, they could have saved themselves all this concern as the answer to where we were going rang out clear in the night in which the *Ayesha* disappeared, in the following words: "To the Rhine, to the Rhine, to the German Rhine; where we all wish to keep guard."[1]

1. Extract from the famous German song, "The Watch on the Rhine."

CHAPTER 14

The Meeting with the Choising

SLOWLY THE *AYESHA* PROCEEDED to sea under light breezes from aft until about 3 o'clock in the morning when we passed beyond Dutch jurisdiction. I had just turned in when Lieutenant Schmidt, who had the watch, woke me, saying, "Captain, a German boat is coming alongside!"

As I knew we were on the high seas, I growled: "Man, quit your fooling; let me sleep!"

He reassured himself that what he had reported was indeed true and I could not resist the strenuous protests. At the same time I heard outboard the loudest noise: "There she is, there she is! We finally managed to catch her!"

Coming on deck I made out a small rowboat manned by a few men coming up out of the night and approaching us as fast as she could. A small hand-bag, followed by one other, flew on deck; the two owners close behind revealing themselves as an officer of the reserve and as a chief machinist's mate of the reserve. Both reported to me for duty. As we were outside Dutch jurisdiction, there seemed to be no reason why I should not ship them in my crew.

The hardest task was the quartering of the officer because

the one bed was not quite sufficient for three. It was therefore arranged so that while one officer slept in the bed in the cabin, the second used the space under the mess table, a place that was not quite safe, while the third officer, that had the watch, sat there at his feet. With an increasingly good breeze we managed by the next evening to reach the already well-known Sea-Flower Channel. Unexpectedly we saw a large steamer heading toward us on an easterly course. As it is impossible to navigate in this unlighted strait and as the more northerly Siberut Strait, which was lighted, was naturally the customary mercantile route, the appearance of a steamer in this locality was exceedingly strange. I concluded therefore that she was a man-o'-war.

As quickly as possible we set every rag we had and steered to starboard in order to try to make the Dutch three-mile limit as soon as possible. Soon the flat, palm-covered coral islands came in sight, easily recognized by the broad white stripes of the ever-roaring breakers. We ran along as closely as we could to the breakers, about a thousand meters from land. We could not anchor, due to the great depth of water, as these islands seem to rise straight up out of the sea. We were not pleased to note that our unknown steamer shortly thereafter carried on a signal conversation in secret code by searchlight with another ship, as yet unseen by us. The second "man-o'-war," of which we were now reasonably certain, soon disappeared toward the south, the first cruised back and forth in the Sea-Flower Channel. As the wind unfortunately gradually died down, our hopes of being out of sight of the cruiser by daylight were not fulfilled.

I concocted the scheme of steering among the numerous islands, tying the *Ayesha* up to a strong palm, taking down top masts and sails, so that we could not be discovered from the sea. Then I grew curious to know the character of the ship. The light breezes however spoiled this plan. We were only a few miles away from the man-o'-war as the sun rose, and hardly had the masts of the *Ayesha* appeared in the light, when the man-o'-war came about sharply and set her course for us at high speed. We were still within the three-mile limit and had no idea of leaving this protection. Luckily we discovered that this man-o'-war was neither English nor Japanese, but the Dutch flagship *The Seven Provinces*. Remaining at a great distance the armored ship followed us until we passed their limits of jurisdiction, bound westward.

We proceeded with the *Ayesha* to sea, endeavoring to make a predetermined position in the ocean. There we hoped to meet a German steamer. We could not make any definite plans with the German ships lying in Padang; but their captains knew, from the ship-to-ship conversation, what course we would take. We understood that one of the steamers would follow us out and make our further cruising an easy matter. In this way we cruised around for about three weeks. Likewise we had to endure some heavy weather which the pigs did not like, they being quartered in a pen built around the capstan up in the bow. In order to lighten the existence of these animals and help them because of the heavy rolling, we nailed strips across the deck so that they would not slide about from one side to the other.

Twice our hopes of an approaching steamer were blasted. Each time it was an English ship. One of these carried on so peculiarly and went through the most remarkable maneuvers at our approach, that we thought she must be working in conjunction with some auxiliary cruiser. Therefore we cleared ship for action. In order to give the steamer something to think about and to further our attempts at disguising ourselves as a harmless sailing ship, we made the signal: "Please give us the longitude." A signal that is more or less customary for a sailing ship to address to a steamer when they meet at sea. She gave us the required answer, but added the tormenting question: "Who are you?" We had no identification flags and we did not wish to give the ship's signal as described in the ship's papers. We therefore took four very beautiful flags, secured them together, tied a knot in each of the two upper flags so that nobody could possibly read them and hoisted the signal, half hidden by a sail. So the steamer would think that we had answered her question and she merely could not make it out. About a half hour later the steamer disappeared. Her return signal was still flying, "I can see your signal, but cannot make it out." The second English steamer was so far away that she could hardly have seen us.

The 14th of December, 1914, was a rainy, misty day with a fairly heavy sea. *Ayesha* lay to under few sails. Suddenly there appeared out of the mist a steamer with two masts and one smoke-pipe about 4000 meters on the port hand, steering an easterly course. We were steering westerly. The usual courses of merchantmen in this locality are either north or south. So if a steamer is found here steering east, it certainly must be for a special reason. And the truth of this assertion was actually proved as it turned out to be a German steamer looking for us.

We therefore steered for her, carried all possible sail, shot white and red stars that could also be seen in daylight, in order to attract the steamer's attention which we by now recognized as the Lloyd liner *Choising*. Our greatest anxiety was the fear that *Choising* would not make us out in the misty weather and would pass on by. Finally, after the fourth or fifth star had been fired, we knew that she had discovered us and was heading in our direction.

We hoisted our flag and pennant on high. The steamer also hoisted the German flag. Our men climbed into the shrouds and three cheers were exchanged between ships. My men were dressed in their normal "Paradise" boarding costumes. The *Choising* crew afterwards told us that they were very much surprised to see a sailing ship, rigging filled with naked forms, bob up out of the mist. It was impossible to get aboard *Choising* in the heavy seaway. As I had come up from the south where we had better weather, I signalled the *Choising* to follow us.

The next day the weather grew worse instead of better and

during the night a heavy storm was raging. Very little sail was carried by *Ayesha*. We had to trust to the ship to take up its own position in order to ride out the blow. None of the "seas" succeeded in breaking over the *Ayesha* as she rode them like a duck. She was wet, however, both in and out, the spray continually sweeping the decks.

At daylight the *Choising*, a 1700-ton gross ship, signalled, "Because of the storm I cannot remain in the open sea." I then decided to run for the lee of the land and there attempt to effect the transfer, signalling *Choising* a new rendezvous. The two ships parted company again because I had to take a different course with the sailing ship than the steamer had to take.

The following night was the worst we experienced aboard the *Ayesha*. The storm raged the entire night. We were in the neighborhood of the islands, but we did not know our exact position. The storm and wind threatened to drive us on the reefs. The night was so pitch dark that we could see nothing. Should we, in a case like this, get too near the beach it would be the end of both ship and crew. Even the small rags, the close-reefed sails, that we still carried were entirely too much. Toward morning an exceptionally heavy squall came along. The old sails were not equal to this. One crash and then another crash, our foresail and storm jib ripped to pieces and only a few small flying rags whipped in the breeze. The flying foresail took along a third sail, the fore stay sail, so that we were now bereft of all sails up forward. Owing to the darkness and the heavy sea it was impossible to break out the reserve sails. With our after sails we had to come about and lay to, trusting to our luck to keep us out of the breakers.

As the gray dawn came on, we broke out the reserve sail and bent them on. Shortly thereafter the wind fell. We could then increase sail and head for the appointed rendezvous with the *Choising*. As we were in that neighborhood, about 9 A.M. the *Choising* came in sight in the distance. In the meantime it became so calm that the *Ayesha* lost practically all headway. I therefore signalled the *Choising* to take us in tow and proceed to the lee of the next island. There we were sheltered from the wind and sea and the shifting over could be carried out.

CHAPTER 15

The Ayesha's End

WHILE BEING TOWED BY the *Choising* we began to dismantle the good old *Ayesha*. We were, unfortunately, forced to sink her as we had no harbor in which to send her. Had we taken her into a Dutch harbor, the danger remained of her being eventually returned to her former owners. Above all things, we had to prevent that. All the remaining provisions and all the weapons were gathered together on deck. We had no further use for handbags. The galleon picture of *Ayesha*, that represented the favorite wife of the prophet, was unscrewed and taken down, as was also the steering wheel, and taken along aboard the *Choising* as mementos.

Soon we got in close behind the sheltering island and the heavy swells calmed down so that it was possible to take the *Ayesha* alongside the steamer. Meantime the *Ayesha*'s shrouds, that is, the ropes that support the masts, were cut and all stays, etc., were removed and destroyed. At the same time two large holes were bored through the ship in the storeroom so that she gradually began to fill.

About 4 o'clock that afternoon we turned over the *Choising*'s engines and the *Ayesha* was cast adrift. It seemed as if the ship did not wish to part with us. Although the *Choising* was going ahead and there were no lines attached to the *Ayesha*, she remained alongside for quite a while. As if the *Ayesha* finally realized that her strength was failing, she attempted to hold on by cutting into us abaft the gangway and tried to take a piece along with her.

I wished to remain near the *Ayesha* until she sank. So we stopped the engines and lay off about 300 to 400 meters. The loss of the heroic old ship touched our hearts. Although life aboard her was anything but pleasant we still realized that we had the *Ayesha* to thank for our freedom. For almost a month and a half she was our home, covering 1709 sea-miles under sail in that time. Standing aft along the stern rail we all watched her in her last battle with the waves. Slowly and gradually she sank deeper and deeper. Soon the water covered the main deck. Then suddenly she gave a last gasp as the entire vessel trembled. The bow seemed to rise up out of the water for the last time and then dove down deeply. The iron ballast having shifted forward, the *Ayesha* stood up perpendicularly, rudder on high, masts even with the water, and then shot like a stone down into the depths, never to appear again. "three hurrahs" were given for her over her watery grave.

This occurred at 4.58 P.M., December 16, 1914.

Aboard the *Choising*, I set a westerly course and then began the work of quartering the men. The ship's crew were already settled in a former coal bunker which had been cleaned out for this purpose. There were also sufficient covers, mattresses, etc., so that, in comparison with the *Ayesha*, we seemed to be leading a regular carousing sort of life.

My new ship was not a speedy one. On occasions she could be forced to 7½ knots, but, as we later discovered, we had to be satisfied with 4 knots. In part, this was due to poor coal. The *Choising* was one of the steamers that had previously been designated as a collier to the *Emden*. She had waited a very long time at the rendezvous for the *Emden*. As the British Admiralty was so amiable as to unselfishly anticipate the *Em-*

den's wishes and provide her with Welsh coal, evidently destined for Hong Kong, there arose no need for the *Emden* to take the poor Indian and Australian coal with which the *Choising* was loaded and awaiting. In the course of this waiting the *Choising* used this cargo as fuel so that we now had to use the half-burned coal that still remained on hand.

We also received some news on the *Choising*. On leaving Padang in the *Ayesha* I could not determine where to proceed first. My first plan, to proceed to Tsing tau, was dropped when I heard in Padang that it had fallen into the enemy's hands. Then I planned to intercept H.M.S. *Königsberg*. I knew only that she was supposed to be cruising in the Indian Ocean. In case I heard that she was no longer there, and I expected news on the *Choising*, I intended to head for German East Africa. We knew that an engagement had taken place there between the German colonial guard and the English. After some further reflection I gave up this scheme, as even the success of this undertaking would not produce adequate results. A force of 50 men, themselves in need of an outfit of clothing and possessing nothing which the soldiers would need, such as a doctor, medical supplies, knowledge of the language, guides, charts, etc., it was decided that it was impossible to effect a junction with a military force of only several thousand men in a war-ridden country of the size of South East Africa. There remained no alternative but to circle Africa and head for home. However, the question of re-provisioning made this a difficult matter.

Finally we found an article in the newspapers dealing with a fight between the Turks and the English at Scheik Seid, that is near Perim (Bab-el-Mandeb—The Gate of Suffering). The notice seemed to insinuate that the war had also engulfed Turkey. And so we discovered, after some further searching in the newspapers, the report of the declaration of war between England and Turkey. Therefore Arabia seemed foremost in our minds as our proper destination. I decided to head for that place. The still feasible plan of hunting the *Königsberg* had not been abandoned until the *Choising* brought news that she had been sunk in a fight to the northward of Australia, and a second report that the *Königsberg* had been trapped in the Rufigi River and was now blockaded. In case she had been sunk there would be no further use of hunting her, and in case she really were blockaded, then she needed coal and we could not bring her any coal. The 50 men that I would add to her complement would only be 50 more eaters.

At first I lay the *Choising* on southerly courses to avoid the main steamer routes and at the same time to keep clear of the dangers of tropical cyclones. For such a cyclone the *Choising* was not constructed. In order to be sure to sight enemy ships before they saw us, we maintained a very sharp lookout. Had we met a man-o'-war the only hope of safety lay in a bluff at our enormous speed.

Choising was still painted as a Lloyd liner—black sides, white rail and spar color superstructure. Of course we could not proceed any further in this condition, so we painted her to look like a Hollander. Then we thought that in the Straits of Bab-el-Mandeb we would no doubt meet other vessels and we would have the same tormenting question asked of us, "Who are you?" Other than the English list aboard, we had no ship's registry. Finally, however, we found therein names of several steamers that were sold by English owners to foreigners. One of these was a 1700-ton gross steamer, named *Schenir,* that had been sold to Genova. As she was, on the whole, of an appearance similar to the *Choising,* we rechristened our ship and shortly thereafter, in large white letters, the following inscription appeared on her stern: *"Schenir*—Genova."

This discovery in the English list was particularly pleasing as I was most anxious to cruise as an Italian. Because of the swaying policy of Italy I could rest assured that even an English warship would take good care not to unnecessarily inconvenience an Italian ship.

The *Schenir* out of Genova must of course fly the Italian

flag which, unfortunately, was not to be found on board. Neither was there any green bunting, so we took a green window curtain and sewed a piece of white and red bunting on it. A committee, with abilities in the art line, was appointed and went to work to paint the proud Italian crest on the white field. The green color of the window curtain did not seem to be quite the proper shade. As we had a pot of yellow and a pot of blue paint aboard, we mixed them to get the correct shade of green and then hung the flag (as much as necessary of it) in the pot.

CHAPTER 16

From Perim to Hodeida

O N JANUARY 7, 1915, WE HAVE ARRIVED IN the vicinity of Perim Straits. Nothing of importance happened at sea. Several steamers hove in sight and were safely passed. I always changed course so as to appear to be heading toward Africa. We kept on that course as long as the steamer was in sight and then went back to our proper course again.

The Christmas celebration was very quiet, but New Year's a little more lively, as we made a clean sweep of the remaining stock of the *Choising*'s beer and wine.

I had intended to enter the Straits of Perim at nightfall. Again I was unfortunate because we had no charts. As in the case of entering Padang, we had also this time to draw our own charts of the Red Sea, and, naturally, we were not quite clear as to where the ships were usually expected to be found. Therefore I came to the entrance of the straits several hours too early. So I gave orders to make a big sweep and then cruise back and forth. A large steamer coming out of Dschibuti gave us a few anxious moments because we mistook it for a man-o'-war. Actually, however, it was a French mail packet. At nightfall we again headed in, and, making all possible speed, entered the straits.

I took it for granted that some kind of a watch would be maintained (by the English). The *Choising* was practically helpless before even the smallest warship. It was even impossible to run away, as any sort of steam craft could overhaul us. It seemed necessary, therefore, to once more lead my crew into action; the steamer had to be operated with this end in view.

In case of being intercepted by the enemy near the African coast I determined to run ashore and to land my crew in the ship's boats. Under those circumstances we would be landing on enemy territory and would be free and unhampered to move as we pleased. In case we were taken on the north side of the straits, I would boldly and fearlessly enter Perim harbor, or, failing that, drive the steamer into the mud and attempt to surprise and capture the telegraph station there. In order to prepare for all these emergencies the four large ship's boats of the *Choising* were swung out, lowered to the rail and secured there. In the boats we stowed water and provisions for eight weeks, arms, ammunition and our few necessities. Each officer commanded a boat and the crew were detailed to the boats. The orders for the boats, in case it became necessary, were, once and for all: "Follow the leader."

As it was now dark we again found ourselves uncertain as to our exact location. Outside we had seen a number of small islands lying across the entrance of the straits which we took to be the "Seven Brothers." Actually they were the high Arabian mountains whose peaks were visible over the horizon. This we found out later when we came in sight of the flashing light of Perim. But this light gave us a good departure for navigating further.

It goes without saying that all hands came on deck as we neared the straits. Everybody peered around very carefully, as faithful watching was our only weapon. The vessel was carefully darkened. I had the officers and petty officers make the rounds of the ship over and over again to be sure that absolutely no light was visible from the outside. The Chinese crew of the *Choising* little understood the meaning of this precaution. Whether I should or should not darken the ship was a matter of careful consideration. If I showed the usual few lights as customarily carried by merchantmen it might be possible that the police ships of the English would pass me by as not worthy of consideration. A darkened ship, however, in case we were seen, would be sure to arouse suspicion. In the end I decided to darken her.

The Straits of Bab-el-Mandeb are very narrow. I squeezed the ship over as closely as possible to the African coast because there the horizon was darker and the land also gave a darker background to the ship. In spite of that we came close to the lighthouse of Perim, so that in the space where we turned we were constantly lighted up every second as if by a searchlight. Close to Perim we could see two English men-o'-war signalling to each other in Morse. Many curses were heaped on our engines in the next half hour because they could make only 7½ knots. Luck was with us however. The Englishmen did not see us. Perhaps also, the small patrol boats, which I expected, were not on their stations that night as we had a high wind and also a fairly high sea. After two long drawn-out hours we considered ourselves "through."

For the remainder of the trip in the Red Sea I kept off the usual steamer track, and about dark on January 8 stood in toward Hodeida.

The only book that we could use as a guide to instruct us in the Arabian customs was a "World's Trip" book belonging to the *Choising*'s doctor, that was probably an excellent work on "honeymoon" trips. In this we read that Hodeida was a large commercial city and that the Hedshas Railroad was being constructed to Hodeida. As this book was several years old, and as one of my officers told of having met a French engineer several years ago who had been working on the construction of the Hodeida Railroad, we supposed that by this time the road must be about completed. In case this were not so, we would have to get all the war information we could, also some Red Sea charts, and then proceed further by water.

On nearing Hodeida, or, to be more correct, on nearing the neighborhood where Hodeida was supposed to be—because of our lack of charts we never knew where we were—we suddenly saw a long row of electric lights along the beach. Our rejoicing was great over the first signs of the beginning of civilization. That Hodeida would have electric lights was beyond our expectations.

"That seems to be quite a comfortable nest," was heard on the bridge. "Even electric lights. Then most certainly must the railroad be running. I can see us all getting aboard the special through train at the central station tomorrow morning. In 14 days we shall be on the North Sea." The lights were assumed to be on the dock, as our "World's Trip" guide-book said there was a harbor there. On closer approach my suspicions became aroused. I soon saw that the lights were peculiarly disarranged (not symmetrical) as is seldom seen on a dock. As we were very sober, the defect must be with the dock. I stopped the ship to take a sounding in order to find out approximately how far off the beach we were. The sounding showed 40 meters. We were now only a few thousand meters from the supposed-to-be dock, but, according to the sounding, we were several miles off shore. With this knowledge, the dock lost considerable attraction for us. It must be something else. So I gave the orders "course south," and we ran away for several miles.

Then I lowered the four boats into the water, which remained ready since our passage by Perim. My crew embarked in the boats. I gave the captain of *Choising* orders to proceed out to sea, lie at a predetermined rendezvous well off the mercantile routes, to return each of the two following nights to the same place where I was leaving him and wait for me. In case I did not return, he was to proceed to Massaua. The reason I directed the steamer to return twice more was because

I did not then know who controlled South Arabia. My last information was three months old and then I merely knew that the English and Turks were at war. Of the results of this war I knew nothing. Therefore it was quite possible that Hodeida was in English hands. In case I planned to proceed further along the next night in the *Choising*. During the day I intended to hide any place in the desert. At the same time I arranged so that in case I heard of any enemy ships that endangered the *Choising* I would let her know by signal by hand lantern: "Enemy ships in neighborhood. Proceed to Massaua." I did not wish to place the *Choising* in any danger of being recaptured before she could get started back.

The *Choising* soon disappeared into the black of the night while my small flotilla rowed in company in the direction of the beach. As in the case of all boats that have not been waterborne for some time, the *Choising*'s boats leaked very badly, even though I had, several days previously, sprayed the boats inside and out, filled them half full of water and then given them a new coat of paint. Our attention was, therefore, now riveted on the necessity of bailing out the boats. At daybreak I had my flotilla set sail, which then developed into a real race for the shore.

Our "dock" doused its lights, and at sunrise we could see its bridge, two masts and four smoke-pipes, fully armed and armored, that was named *Desaix*. It was a French armored cruiser. Another part of the dock was discovered to be the Italian ship *Juliana*. We had no intention of landing at that sort of dock so we turned toward the beach.

The greatest anxiety lay in the fact that the armored cruiser might discover us. One of my boats was Chinese rigged, the other three German rigged. Four boats, painted gray, with such unusual rigs must certainly, in this neighborhood, lead to an investigation. On nearing land I anchored and had all the boats brought alongside my boat and secured. Masts and sails were stowed away while we discussed what to do next. *Choising* had gone away. Behind us were the French armored

cruiser and the Italian ship. We had no information as to
Italy's position. Before us along the coast lay the breakers. We
had to practically admit that this portion of Arabia must now
be in French hands. To remain in the boats was impossible,
as in the course of the day we should most certainly be discovered by the Frenchmen who were now still asleep. I
therefore ordered "Ashore!"

Luckily we rode through the breakers with our heavily
laden boats without either capsizing or swamping the boats.
On the way in we met an Arabian fishing boat, and in answer
to our questions, the Arab calmly informed us that Hodeida
was in French hands. The error came about through the following situation: We spoke fairly good German and the Arab
exercised complete mastery over the Arabian tongue, but in
spite of that a satisfactory linguistic intercourse was not absolutely guaranteed. Our boats grounded just behind the
breakers, but about 800 meters from the beach. All our equipment had to be carried ashore through this long stretch of
knee-deep water. We hurriedly built some rafts out of masts,
oars, boards, life preservers and such, and upon these we
placed our munitions, machine guns, etc., in order to make
the transportation ashore all the more rapidly. First we landed
the machine guns.

I waded through immediately. An Arab was splashing
about in the water near the shore. Making every sign of good
will and friendship of which I was capable, and without weapons, I approached him in order to shake his hand. He misunderstood me however and drew back. The same thing happened to a second one who had approached in the meantime.
While I was busy attending to the job of getting our equipment ashore another approached on a camel. He was in uniform. The uniform was blue and red. His head was wrapped
up in a cloth (turban). Possibly he was a Frenchman. This
man, to my discomfort, was armed. Approaching to within
about 600 meters he remained stock-still, his gun swung clear

ready for use, watching our work. Without arms, I approached him, beckoned to him, yelled at him and made signs of every kind and description to convince him that I wished to speak to him. Up to about 200 meters he allowed me to proceed, then he aimed at me. I stood still. He lowered his piece. Then I advanced several paces. He again aimed at me. I stood still and he again lowered his gun. I again advanced a few paces. He again aimed at me. I stood still—and so this irksome performance was repeated for several minutes until I had gained about 50 more meters in his direction. Then he did not again lower his piece, and as a result, I stood standing a little longer. It was impossible for him to understand my talk. He understood none of my calls. He made a sign that could not be misconstrued as anything else but for us to remain there. I most earnestly assured him that we had no intention of leaving, that we were very well off where we were, and then I returned. He climbed aboard his camel and disappeared at full speed in the direction of Hodeida whose white houses we could make out in the distance.

Now it was high time to hurry. In three or four hours we would have the entire French garrison on our necks. Therefore we worked with the greatest energy to get our gear ashore and take up the march into the desert. I intended to remain in the desert during daylight and at night send an officer into Hodeida to get the news. In case the news were bad I would remain in the desert another day and then, on the following night, intercept the *Choising* and get on my way scouting for better luck.

Just as we were about to start marching, a host of armed Bedouins, eighty, a hundred and then more, streamed over the low sand-hills of the desert. They deployed into some form of firing-line and then hid themselves behind the sand-dunes. At the same time we also formed our firing-line and cleared for action. I waited for the first shot to come from the other side. After a few minutes about 12 of these figures, unarmed, disengaged themselves from the enemy firing-line and approached us, waving to us with their arms. I unbuckled my saber and revolver and went to meet them.

We met in the middle between the two lines. A most violent discussion thereupon ensued. Unfortunately, however, neither understood the other. The Bedouins yelled, they gesticulated wildly as only a southerner can, and made the most remarkable signs, all without my being able to understand what they wanted. My attempts to converse with them in German, English, French or Malayan all failed. I therefore had the war flag, which we carried along, brought up to them and showed them in my most eloquent hand sign language, the black, white, red, the iron cross, the eagle. They did not understand it. With a suspicion that the natives of the coast in any locality where I might be forced to land would not recognize our war flag, I took the precaution to bring along a large merchant flag. This I then showed them. And neither did they recognize that. Then we pointed toward the French armored cruiser lying in the harbor, shook our fists at it in the wildest manner and yelled at the same time "Bum, bum bum!" But they always returned with their crazy signs. They held their hands umbrella-fashion in front of their foreheads and at the same time lustily wagged their heads from left to right, or they stroked across their faces with two fingers, either above or below. A further sign was the rubbing together of the outstretched fore-finger of each hand, meantime dumbly gaping at us. That sign we thought we understood. We thought, "there is friction between two," that is, "we are enemies." We attempted by every manner or means that we could possibly think of to make it clear to them that this was not the case. We had no need of all this explanation, because, as we later discovered, the sign did not mean "we are *enemies*," but instead it meant "we are *friends*." As a last resort we drew forth a gold piece. To this form of conversation the Arabs were very susceptible. We showed them the eagle. They of course did not understand that at all. Then we showed them the Kaiser's picture. This aroused their liveliest interest, and finally, from their side the word dribbled out—"Aleman." That was understood on our side. It could mean nothing but "German." Therefore we all yelled at the top of our lungs, as is customary in that country: "Aleman! Aleman!" And thereby did we effect an understanding.

In reply, there arose on the side of the Arabs a lusty and enthusiastic yell. The guns were stowed away, and the whole gang surrounded us, crying and yelling and tearing around, carrying our heavy equipage, dragging our machine guns and such. With a great uproar the calvacade set out in the direction of Hodeida. One of the brothers could speak a little broken English and from him I learned that Hodeida was in Turkish hands.

Our party created much commotion. Although the desert through which we travelled seemed devoid of people, it nevertheless harbored a great number. In this country every youngster of 12 years shoulders a gun and is a soldier. Very shortly another crowd of perhaps several hundred Bedouins came up and wanted to fire on us, thinking we were enemies. Our hundred guides made energetic signs, accompanied by much yelling and howling, to make it clearly understood to their hundred other colleagues that we were friends. After they had then finished their demonstrations of joy we proceeded with 200 guides a little further until, a half hour later, 200 more came up, wished to engage us thinking we were enemies, were harangued by our 200 guides until they also understood that we were friends.

These demonstrations were always accompanied by a considerable loss of time. And thus it became noon. We had had nothing to eat since the previous evening and in the meantime we had worked hard and had already walked a long stretch in the glowing hot sand at a time of day when one usually avoids even riding in the sun. They had eventually thoroughly grasped the fact that we were German and so they carried on like clowns; danced, sang, yelled, fired their guns and indulged in all sorts of tomfoolery.

Meanwhile the first Turkish officers came out of Hodeida, among them several who spoke German. The mutual pleasure was very great, and accompanied by some more high jinks with their rifles. The whole Turkish garrison had been drawn up against us, as they expected to have to repulse an enemy landing force. Even the guns were trained on us. Between the Turkish troops, with flags flying, we made our entry into Hodeida. The civil population stood in the streets and applauded us, and, whenever one of our marching songs that we sang ended, there followed loud yelling and applause.

My men were quartered in a barracks, quickly made ready for them. The officers were allotted a house in town previously secured for this purpose. Everything was provided for us. Looking from our house we could see the French cruiser several miles away, rocking, as in peaceful slumber, on the blue sea.

CHAPTER 17

To Sanaa

AVING SEEN MY MEN quartered, I left about 5 P.M., January 9, to consult with the chief civil and military authorities in regard to my future movements. There were two ways open to reach Germany; the first, to proceed overland, and the second, to continue cruising at sea. Charts could be obtained in Hodeida. The governor of Hodeida, His Excellency, Raghib, and the colonel of the regiment, also named Raghib, sat with me in consultation that afternoon.

To my dismay I was now authoritatively informed that the railroad was not completed. Then I received information in regard to the disposition of English men-o'-war in the Red Sea. These consisted mainly of gunboats and auxiliary cruisers that could be seen daily maintaining a blockade to the northward of Hodeida. The get-away in the *Choising* under these circumstances offered little hope of success as we had to count on the fact that the French cruiser would certainly be informed by spies of our presence in Hodeida. She would then take up the search for our steamer, and by radio notify all the other English and French warships. It was therefore impossible for a ship of the 7½-knot *Choising* class to break through in such narrow waters as the Red Sea. The Turkish authorities however assured me that it was perfectly safe for me to march overland to the north even though it would take some time. Preparations for this march would take about 14 days, but then I could start off and reach a railroad in about two months.

As soon as this had been agreed upon I went to the roof of my house at twilight and sent the *Choising* three times the previously agreed upon signal by lantern, "Attention! Enemy warships! Proceed to Massaua immediately!" Later on we heard that the *Choising* had safely reached her destination. Although up to this time my men had remained in excellent health, they now began to show the effects of this unfavorable weather. In Hodeida the days are glowing hot, the nights quite cool. The men slept in the Turkish barracks along with the Turkish soldiers.

In South Arabia, the houses and barracks are built very differently from those in our climate. The barracks in which my men were quartered consisted of wooden frames covered over with matting and straw. They slept close together on a long sort of divan which was upholstered with straw. The water was so unhealthy that only boiled water could be used for drinking purposes. Quinine was taken constantly to ward off malaria. In spite of these precautions cases of dysentery and malaria cropped out. I decided, therefore, to leave with my men and go up to the mountains. The city of Sanaa, principal city of Yemen, was recommended as being very healthy, especially was the water-supply said to be excellent, the climate closely resembling that of Europe. My route overland would take me via Sanaa anyway, and I could just as well await there the completion of my preparations for the march. So I decided to start the march toward Sanaa on the Kaiser's birthday.

Even way down in Hodeida the Kaiser's birthday was celebrated, the whole Turkish garrison and the total Turk-Arabian population taking part. I had meanwhile managed to fit my men out in new clothes, and even though these uni-

forms did not quite conform to the official uniform regulations, especially in regard to the new tropical helmet with its
black-white-red cockade which previously had not been
adopted by the navy, they managed to make a neat appearance
and a very excellent impression. The whole garrison was
drawn-up on the parade ground to celebrate. My men stood
in the middle of the Turkish troops. Accompanied by the
Turkish colonel I stepped out in front of the allied line, made
my speech for the Kaiser in the German language, concluding
with three cheers for the Kaiser, in which our Turkish Allies
joined vociferously. After the Kaiser speech another speech
was made, this time by the Turkish colonel, in honor of the
Sultan. A public parade closed the ceremonies. With music
and waving flags my men returned to their barracks for a
banquet—mutton and rice—in the palace of the chief mayor
of Hodeida. We also exchanged the most cordial toasts. The
departure toward Sanaa took place about 5 o'clock that afternoon.

In the Arabian desert it is impossible to travel except by
night as it is too hot for man and beast in the day time.
Marching afoot is also impossible, and even at night one has
to ride. In this way we had to proceed until we arrived at the
base of the mountains.

We were provided with horses, mules and asses for the trip.
Our equipage was transported by a caravan of camels. At the
beginning it was rather difficult to keep my newly organized
band together as many of my young bluejackets were now
aboard four-legged animals for the first time in their lives.
The most amusing sights began at the very outset with
mounting. Some of the men used their spare time before departure to practice quick dismounting, each getting accustomed to his own saddle. Finally each managed to get on
friendly terms with his own beast so that I did not have to
bother about exceptional straggling any longer, and the caravan set forth, accompanied for a stretch by the Turkish officers and Turkish garrison.

Hodeida was soon left behind and we were now in the middle of the desert. As far as the eye could see was nothing but sand (low, flat sand-hills), on which grew tough grass. Roads, of course, did not exist. The only guide was the trail left in the sand by previous caravans. During the march we frequently had to stop, as naturally, every instant or two, one of my men would not be able to control his mount. The duel, which always followed, invariably ended with the throwing of the rider. Then it was necessary to recapture the beast, over-joyed with his freedom, a job which usually fell to the officers as they were the only ones who could ride. It was not a simple matter to capture the mules and asses. As one approached them they would turn around and kick out most energetically with their hind legs so that it was usually necessary to resort to tricks and ruses to capture them. In order to prevent a great loss of time an officer was detailed to ride in rear of the caravan. He gathered in all the riderless-mules and muleless-riders and formed a small rear guard. As it was a moonlight night we had no trouble in keeping to the trail. We rode the entire night, taking a few half hour pauses. During these pauses we threw ourselves down where we stood, held the bridles over our arms (or else hobbled the critters), and in this way rested our weary limbs that had grown very stiff in this tiresome riding.

The country through which we rode is not absolutely safe. Robberies and the looting of caravans are daily occurrences. This we found out during our second night. Suddenly we saw in the moonlight across the trail about a dozen camel riders. The Turkish guides accompanying us declared them to be robbers and made their rifles ready. As the camel riders saw the strength of our caravan they dusted, disappearing among the sand-hills.

On the third day we had completed the trip across the desert and were now approaching the mountains. These mountains seem to suddenly rise straight up out of the desert.

They are about 3600 meters high. The going was now getting heavier. Over rocky hills, through flooding rivers and beds of streams we made slow headway toward the mountains. Finally we again saw trees and bushes, the vegetation becoming more luxuriant. The Arabs living here had endeavored to build their houses in high, inaccessible places. Wherever a stone projection jutted out, or wherever a small, steep mountain road made the approach difficult, there were imposing Arabian towns, each a small fortress in itself. We imagined we had been suddenly transported back to the middle ages.

The inhabitants seemed friendly and greeted us on all sides. The hours of resting were usually spent in the houses prepared in advance for the use of Turkish troops. We marched through a picturesque mountain country for a few days until we came face to face with a mountain ridge that seemed to absolutely block our way so that we knew not which way to proceed. It was a vertical, stone covered wall. A difficult serpentine path led us to the top of the spur after hours of climbing. The path was not entirely without danger. On one side the mountain rose perpendicularly; on the other side it fell perpendicularly. It was impossible, for one's peace of mind, to ride up this path. It was worn in the side of the mountains, among huge boulders and rolling stone, by many years of use as a mule track.

The carrying capacity and strength of the pack animals was astounding. Often we came to places so dangerous that I ordered the luggage taken off them and had the animals led over by hand. By this time my men had learned to ride with considerable proficiency. We could buy eggs and milk whenever we needed them. Having carried our mess gear with us on a pack mule, I detailed an officer, accompanied by the cook and one other man, to ride on ahead because it is always easier for a small caravan to march faster than a large one. Also we found our food prepared in advance when we arrived. This was a great pleasure to the men because the trip was so strenuous that every hour of rest was given up to heavy sleeping. Ever since we reached the mountains we rode by day and slept by night.

I had planned a longer halt at Menacha. This is a small city located at the highest elevation of the principal mountain spur. From there the road gradually descends to a large high plane on which Sanaa is built. At Menacha we were received most enthusiastically by the Turkish garrison and civil populace. Many hours before our arrival there, we were met by the commander and his officers and troops. Also a crowd, numbering in the hundreds, came out to meet us. Together with the Turkish forces we covered the last stretch of road, preceded by a huge crowd of Arabs, picturesquely clad, carrying on foolishly in their own way and dancing to the tune of their own songs.

We were received most royally in Menacha. Because of the storms, the houses here are made of stone. My men were conducted to a large barracks where the best of everything had been prepared for them. A most appetizing and sumptuous meal was awaiting them. The officers were assigned to a hotel, the only hotel in all Arabia that I have ever heard mentioned. This had the additional advantage of real beds. Up to this time we had been sleeping on so called "Cursis," that is, wooden frames covered with matting. The altitude of Menacha is about 3400 meters. We were usually above the clouds. The days were cool, the nights bitterly cold.

We remained in Menacha two days. I utilized this time, while visiting in their houses, to memorize several different Arabian expressions. The Arabian rooms are white throughout, while the window-panes are a variegated assortment of blue, yellow and red. Along the walls are low, comfortable divans and cushions. In the middle of the room, on a carpet, is a brass plate upon which is set the Nargileh (Oriental waterpipe). In accordance with the custom of the land we were always given a cup of Mocha when we visited them and in that way many very pleasant hours of smoking and gossiping were passed with our Arabian hosts.

We again took up our march from Menacha. The Turks were endeavoring to improve their highways in this place; a broad and beautiful, newly laid road, comparing favorably with any European highway, stretched for a long distance away from town. Our journey carried us through wonderful mountain scenery. Most unusual to us was the sight of camels nibbling the tops of the low trees. Frequently we came face to face with hordes of baboons, but in spite of our attempts, we were unable to get a shot at them. The going had improved so much that we could now keep some sort of formation and even indulge in an occasional trot.

On the 7th of March we approached the principal city. From the high passes you could look down on the fertile plain with numerous villages and towns scattered here and there, among which, Sanaa, by reason of its greater size, became easily recognizable. Turkish officers came out to meet us. Outside the town the Turkish garrison was drawn up and received us with music. "Deutschland über Alles" (Germany over all) could be heard. The leading civil and military officials came out on horses and in wagons. The civil populace also rejoiced at our arrival. Even the French consul, interned there, showed himself on the balcony of his house. His British colleague also knew of our arrival which we made known to him while marching in town, but I did not meet him personally. Perhaps he was astonished to hear the strains of "The Watch on the Rhine" floating into his house way up there in the Arabian mountains.

Unfortunately, Sanaa was not as healthy as we had hoped. Because of its altitude alone, the days are bound to be extraordinarily cold. One got accustomed to the climate only after a long residence there. Several days after our arrival 80 per cent of my men were on the sick list with fever, and especially did we all have cramps in the stomach and symptoms of colds.

The city of Sanaa is very interesting. It is composed of three separate districts: the Jewish, the Arabian and the Turkish. A high limestone wall surrounds the entire town as a protection. Inside this wall each of the above-mentioned districts built its own wall making itself a small separate fort. And inside of even these, each house is its own fort. All the streets and roads are lined with high walls, something after the fashion of German trenches, so that from certain points a raking fire can be delivered the whole length of the road. This construction had been caused by the uncertainty as to who really had held the authority. The Yemen province had been known as the most restless province of Turkey and a few years back engagements between the Turks and Arabs were daily occurrences. Frequently the garrisons of the town were besieged. Sanaa was surrendered by the Arabs only after a 10 year starving-out siege. Since then, however, peace and quiet have prevailed throughout the land. After we had been in Sanaa 14 days I found that the hardships of an overland march were so severe that I could not go ahead with my troop. The sickness of my men compelled me to remain there 14 more days without accomplishing anything. At the end of this time, although still weak, they had sufficiently recovered to enable them to mount their animals, and we started on our return trip to Hodeida in order to try once more our luck on the sea.

CHAPTER 18

The Shipwreck

THE RETURN FROM SANAA was accomplished without interruption in the same manner as the march approaching that place. I went on ahead with a few men in order to hurry the preparations for another cruise at sea. I reached Hodeida about a day and a half ahead of the remainder. We managed to make the caravan trip in eight days. We rode day and night with very few pauses. Only when the animals had to be changed did we stop. As we had sent the *Choising* away, and as it was impossible to rake up any more steamers, the only way to leave Hodeida seemed to be by means of "zambuks." These are the small, open sailing vessels, rigged as "dhaus," used along this coast.

I succeeded in unearthing two zambuks at Hodeida, each about 14 meters long and 4 meters beam. These were gathered together in a small bight to the northward of Hodeida, called Jabana. Because of the French armored cruiser, which still maintained its permanent and sleepy watch, it was impossible for me to start from Hodeida. She might possibly wake up. Knowing that the country swarmed with English and French spies, I spread the rumor that I intended to sail from the bight at Isa on March 12. The expected actually happened. On the afternoon of March 12, for the first time since the beginning of the war, an English gunboat appeared in the forlorn Isa bight, which boasted neither house, tree, blade of grass nor water, and examined the beach for us with its searchlight. The poor fools, what would they not have given to have really known where we actually were!

On March 14, about 5 P.M., my squadron left Jabana. The battle-flag flew at the stern of my proud flagship, and, with three cheers to His Majesty the Kaiser, we started the cruise. Lieutenant Gerdis commanded the second flagship. Strict discipline took the place of the other absent ships of the squadron.[1] As the other zambuk was a little larger than mine, I had the sick men put aboard that one. Malaria, dysentery and typhoid still bothered the men, and I had several whose health was such as to cause me not a little uneasiness. I was unwilling, however, to leave my sick behind, as I was certain that nothing but a change of climate would improve them.

I managed to get all the latest information, such as it was, concerning the English, and I therefore knew that the English blockading ships, two gunboats and the auxiliary cruiser *Empress of Russia*, were maintaining a line of blockade from Loheiya over to Kamaran, Jebel Zebayir to Jebel Zukur. I therefore had to run this blockade with my sailboats. In ordered to prevent both boats from being taken at the same place, I ordered Lieutenant Gerdis to leave me. We had decided upon a rendezvous to the north where each should wait for the other a certain length of time.

Soon the second zambuk disappeared in the gathering darkness. For the first time we now began losing headway and at daybreak it was flat calm. To our great dismay we lay motionless, and at sunrise found ourselves in the exact position where we least wished to be, namely, in the middle of the

---

1. TRANSLATOR'S NOTE.—Rather difficult to properly express this German pun in English.

English blockading line. Any minute the appearance of the tops of English masts could be expected. Our hopes ran low. The calm succeeded in holding us more effectually to this place than any action of the enemy could bring about. But I had not planned my departure for over the "week-end" without an object in view. I was sufficiently familiar with the customs of the English to know that during the week-end, that is, Saturday evening and Sunday, the gentlemen were not keen for work. And so it happened that we were not sighted throughout that whole day.

In the course of the afternoon the breeze set in again and about evening at sundown we could go to sleep with the comfortable reflection that we had, even with two becalmed sailboats, been able to run the English line of blockade.

I continued the journey, with my light draft vessels, between the coral reefs of the Farisan bank. This is a giant coral bank, about 350 sea-miles long, where large ships cannot go, and even small boats are not entirely free from danger. During the next day, my second zambuk came in sight. She received orders to remain with me thereafter.

Life aboard the zambuks was, so to speak, right comfortable. There was not very much room. With the Arabs, who tended ship, the interpreters and pilots, we counted up 35 men per boat, so that in a space 14 meters long by 4 meters wide not much space remained for each individual. In addition, a great deal of room in the boat was given over to provisions, water, munitions and machine guns. As a protection against the glowing heat, we spread woolen blankets overhead during the day, so that at least our heads were kept in the shade. The equipment also was rather meager. In each zambuk a small open fireplace of sheet metal was built in and on this we had to cook for 30 men. We attempted to constantly change our menu with the various means at our disposal, so that on the first day we ate, for example, tough mutton with rice and grease; on the next day, rice, grease and tough mutton; on the third day, grease with tough mutton and rice; and so forth and so on. We were making very slow progress. Frequently we had to contend with calms, adverse winds and currents. We were not spared internal dissensions either. At night they raged most strenuously. Of them, the cockroaches, bugs and lice were especially active. Clothes not actually in use had to be lashed down in order to avoid the danger of having them walk away. As soon as the sun came up, shirts were pulled off and the process of "killing lice" begun. The record was 74 lice in one shirt.

On March 17, I signalled my squadron "I intend to anchor this evening." We had now approached the place where my accompanying pilots declared it impossible, even for our small boats, to navigate at night. About 6 P.M. we were drawing close to the Island of Marka where we intended to anchor. The pilot steered the ship for the anchorage. I, with my zambuk, led the way. The second boat followed at about 200 meters. We had a right stiff breeze and a noticeable sea on, and were glad to get into the lee of the island. But we had not reckoned on our skilful Arabian pilot. He piloted so beautifully that presently we struck a coral reef. Two, three times we hit her hard so that I had the gravest doubts as to whether the boat would stand it. Then we again drew clear (evidently jumped it) and were in deep water once more. I anchored immediately. In order to keep the rear ship from hitting the same reef, I yelled and signalled to her. But she also hit it. She had already arrived in the coral reef, and, when turning around, struck another reef. Noticing her flag being hoisted, I knew by this sign that something serious had happened. Immediately I saw the boat slowly begin to list. From the way the mast shook I knew the ship had hit. In an instant the boat disappeared; only the mastheads inclined backwards out of the water. And this occurred close to sunset.

Night falls very quickly in this place. Ten minutes after sunset it is absolutely dark. There was no moonlight. Immediate help was necessary. We had already hoisted sail on our zambuk. All hands got busy. The anchor was torn out of the ground, and while performing a desperate maneuver, in which we almost struck the reef again, we managed to get clear and hasten to the aid of our comrades. I went as near as possible to the sunken zambuk and anchored. Due to the reefs I had to stand off about 400 meters. We had no boats to communicate with each other. Each zambuk had a so-called dugout (these are very small paddle boats chopped out of tree trunks) that could hold at most two men, and whose use was now a serious question in this high sea. I promptly sent my dugouts over to her.

Meantime it had grown dark. We had a lantern aboard our zambuk. Despite all efforts we could not light the lantern to show our location due to the breeze constantly blowing out the matches. "Bring the torches," I ordered. We had brought along several torches from the *Emden* and *Choising* for just such an emergency. They were brought out and made ready. The fuse worked, but the torches would not light. They had, in the course of months, become too wet.

Soon thereafter I heard voices in the night astern of us. They were the first of the men from the other zambuk who were the first of the men from the other zanbuk who were swimming on past us because they could not see. We yelled and blew our battery whistles to attract their attention and, after several anxious minutes, succeeded in doing so. These men had been swimming away from the other zambuk. They had no other means of knowing which direction to swim, except by means of a star that indicated our general direction. How many men were in the water I had no means of knowing. I was also greatly alarmed because that entire region swarmed with sharks. Above all, I knew not what had become of the sick who were too weak to help themselves. Now, once and for all, it became imperative to have light. As everything else had failed, I had wood gathered together, petroleum poured over it, and without considering the ever-present danger of a large fire in an open boat, I had the fire lighted. We held our torches in the flames until they became sufficiently dry to burn. At the same time we fired some white rockets that we still retained, and which, thank God, functioned properly, even though these rockets would call attention to us from miles around. Finally, the two dugouts returned. They were each paddled by one man and carried a sick man in addition. The remaining sick that could not help themselves were brought back either in the dugouts or were lashed alongside them in the water and towed aboard. At the same time the other swimmers arrived from all sides. Those that could not swim, and there were several, wore life preservers and tried to paddle along as best they could. By and by more returned. Soon we had over 50 men aboard so that my zambuk went down so far in the water that we could not hold any more men. I therefore ordered all superfluous cargo thrown overboard, including provisions and water, in order to lighten the ship and to endeavor to carry all the men. Only weapons, munitions and provisions and water for three days remained aboard.

Meanwhile our torches had almost burned out and I feared that the light would not last long enough to be certain of rescuing all the men from the sunken boat. Only the officers failed to arrive—and with the arrival of the last officer our last torch spluttered out. So now, at least, every man was saved. According to the advices of the officer, the sunken zambuk struck a steep coral reef and held there, and we had only our luck to thank for the fact that the masthead remained above water. It could easily have happened that the zambuk would have slid off the reef and disappeared into the deep. Then most certainly would all the sick have drowned and probably also a great portion of the non-swimmers.

Near us lay another zambuk belonging to the tribe of "Idrisz." The Idrisz is an Arabian clan which is not on good terms with the Turks, and also strongly opposed to the advent of Europeans. This zambuk had also sent her dugout to help my second sunken boat. But as soon as she saw that we were Europeans, which she knew by the tropical helmet of our doctor, she turned around and left us to our fate. As it was rather difficult for me to proceed with an overladen boat containing about 70 men, especially when I considered the condition of our provision supply, I sent our Arabian interpreter to the Idrisz' boat shortly before daylight, to offer them a large sum for the use of their boat for a few days. They absolutely refused, however, stating that not even for £100,000 would they do anything for the dogs of Christians. It would have been an easy matter for me to have taken the zambuk by armed force, which I had planned to do that morning. The whole proceeding, however, was not a pleasant one, as a tormenting political discussion would follow such an act. It resolved itself into a question of using armed force against an ally, even though this small uncivilized part of our ally consisted of a wild tribe.

But the next day our "star shone bright" once again. A stiff and fresh southerly blow came on that made it possible to sail before the wind even with a heavily laden boat, and a speedy journey seemed to be ordained. Therefore I left the Idrisz' boat in peace.

We quickly set to work to rescue what we could from the sunken zambuk. The weapons especially were wanted. During the night the zambuk had sunk deeper. The mast broke off and the ship had capsized on the bottom. By diving we managed to salvage two machine guns, several revolvers and some ammunition. All the other stores, clothes, etc., and unfortunately our entire medical outfit, were lost. The stiff breeze pushed us ahead further that one single afternoon than we would have accomplished in perhaps six days under the preceding conditions.

In the evening we landed at Kunfidda. Here we were received in grand style, and although advance preparations could not have been made for us, nevertheless they hurriedly prepared a Turkish meal which we, according to the customs of this region, quickly devoured without the use of knives, forks, plates, etc. A whole mutton, filled with rice, was set on the table. Eagerly we set to work to tear the flesh from the carcass, meanwhile stuffing handfuls of the rice into our mouths. In Kunfidda we met a Turkish official and his wife who also wished to journey to Constantinople and therefore they joined us. This official later on in the trip performed valuable service as a dragoman, *i.e.,* as interpreter.

Quickly we found a larger zambuk in Kunfidda. We rented this one and started off, all hands in one boat. We reached Lidd in the afternoon of March 24, not having encountered any special dangers. This was the most northerly point of the Farisan bank, among whose coral reefs we had, up to this time, found security from our English searchers. And now our cruise would have to be continued on the open ocean. It was well understood that the English would do everything possible to capture us. In Lidd I happened by chance to be given a letter that had been written by a merchant in Dschidda. He wrote that many English warships were closely blockading Dschidda and that every zambuk that attempted to leave the harbor was searched by the English.

Therefore it was impossible to continue further by water. It was necessary to proceed overland. We remained in Lidd for two days in order to gather the necessary animals and organize a caravan, to arrange for our water supply and to make such other necessary preparations as would enable us to go on ahead.

In Lidd we had our first casualty. A seaman, Keil by name, had been suffering from typhus ever since we arrived at Hodeida. The shock of the shipwreck was too much for his weakened constitution. Above all, he suffered the lack of medical assistance which we had been unable to recently give him as we had lost all our medicines. He died at 3 A.M., March 27. Two of his comrades kept constant watch at his bedside and also later, at his bier. We prepared a small rowboat, sewed the remains in sailcloth and weighted it with stones. The warflag covered the whole. On this we placed his hat and his bared saber. After a short religious ceremony we towed the remains of our comrade out to sea and sank it in deep water. Three volleys were fired over his watery grave. It was impossible to bury him ashore as the fanatical and wild inhabitants would probably have disturbed even the peace of the dead. On March 28, we again took up the march.

CHAPTER 19

The Surprise

IT WAS NOT AN EASY MATTER to procure in Lidd sufficient camels for the journey. Lidd is a very small town of only a few hundred inhabitants and has no commercial relations. In order to make the journey more pleasant, I considered it necessary to call on the Sheik of Lidd. This was the first time a Christian had ever entered the sheik's house.

The arrangements were made by my dragoman. After we had exchanged a few gifts he invited me to dine. His house was a wooden-framed, matting-covered affair without windows. Two divans, covered with skins, were set on the sides of the room. Weapons hung from the walls. The other furnishings of the room consisted of smoking materials. Before the meal we were served with either cups of mokka or something like lemon-sour. The mokka was the Arabian kind, that is, not the beans but the shells of the beans were boiled. The whole concoction is a bitter drink, not very pleasing to the European taste, but out of deference to our host had to be gulped down under any circumstances. While we were still sitting in the room, preparations for the meal were begun.

These commenced with the laying of a fairly large, round, woven straw matting upon the bare earth. Servants then entered and heaped a mountain of rice on the straw mat. A small can of preserved mixed pickles completed the table arrangements. One sat, rather one lay, at the table. For all that, everybody was provided with a spoon. All hands set gayly to work on the rice mountain. Meantime, in front of the house, the meat was being prepared, consisting of a whole roasted sheep. There were no knives and forks. Even the mutton did not appear on the table; instead, the two servants detailed for our service tore chunks of mutton from the sheep with their hands and laid the torn-off pieces on the straw matting before each of us.

During the two days spent in Lidd we succeeded in gathering in about 90 camels. With these we could begin the march. The remaining camels we could pick up on the road the next day, so said the sheik. I bought a large outfit of straw mats which I divided among my people. These later on proved their worth as sunshades. In the evening we formed our caravan and left the place, taking up our march into the desert. A large number of camels carried only equipage, especially water, munitions, machine guns and provisions. The water supply was not satisfactory. I had to count on difficulties which would prevent our replenishing our water supply for days at a time.

A journey with camels is very tedious. Sometimes the camel goes ahead, and, according to its standard, not very fast; but we had a caravan of 90 at first, later on, 110 camels. Except for the officers' camels, which were running singly, the other animals were tied together (in that the snout of the rear animal was connected with the tail of the one forward of it by a line about 4 meters long). A line of camels connected together in such a way could not, of course, proceed at the same speed that a single camel would travel, instead the speed of the whole line was limited by the speed of the slowest camel.

Frequently halts had to be made because the packs slid sideways, the girths had to be replaced, the saddles fell off, and so forth.

We kept to a trail that skirted the sea. The entire region is unsafe. Robberies and caravan attacks occur daily. Since leaving Lidd we carried our guns loaded and ready for action. Luckily for us, the nights were light, due to a full moon. According to rule, we travelled from 4 P.M. until the next morning between 9 and 10, or whenever we reached a place where we intended to rest. The average day's work was approximately 14 to 18 hours' riding. Camels are pacers. The riding, therefore, was quite tiresome. The watering places that we passed were holes about 12 to 14 meters deep, dug down in the desert sand, into which leather bags are lowered in order to draw water. The expression "water" does not mean water according to the European definition of that word. On the ground around the water-holes we frequently saw dog carcasses, sheep skeletons and such. The water was an evil-smelling, brown to black colored hog-wash, full of animals. In any case, it could not possibly be used before boiling. Frequently it had a very salty taste.

We were piloted from Lidd by a Turkish officer and seven gendarmes. Further along we were guided by the Arabian sheik of the territory in which we happened to be; because it is the custom to take the man, responsible for your safety, along with you as hostage. Such measures are not unusual in this region. And so our journey continued without interruption until March 31.

On this day, about 11 A.M., we arrived at a water-hole one day's journey distant from Dschidda. Dschidda was our next goal. At this water-hole we found an officer and 17 gendarmes who had come out from Dschidda as emissaries to greet us for our Turkish allies and the civil population of Dschidda. Also they brought us a bountiful supply of water. We made the usual arrangements at this water-hole, hung our straw mats and woolen blankets over the low bushes and lay down with our heads under these so as, by hook or by crook, to get some shelter from the sun's rays. Cooking began as usual, as soon as we were sheltered. Usually by this time all hands had gathered all the dry wood lying around. Then we immediately built a regular fire and the customary food (rice, and when we had luck, mutton) was prepared at once.

When I saw these men who were sent out from Dschidda, I thought that at last the most dangerous part of our trip was over. We were now again approaching a city in which a strong garrison of 300 men was to be found, so I said to myself that if 17 men could safely travel this distance out from Dschidda, then could I, most certainly, with my 50 men safely travel the same distance in to Dschidda.

This region is inhabited by a clan consisting entirely of direct descendants of the prophet, but nevertheless noted because of its wildness and its thieving proclivities. The name of the region, which is very illustrative, is "Father of Wolves."

As usual we got under way about 4 o'clock in the afternoon. The trail led a distance inland from the sea. The country consisted of nothing but sand-hills. It was never possible to see more than 400 meters away. As soon as we had ridden over one sand-hill, the next immediately cut off a further view. Tufts of tough grass, about 2 feet high, grew all over the hills. Suddenly, on our right hand, well off the caravan trail, appeared about 12 or 15 Bedouins, riding at a brisk trot, and disappeared in the direction from which we had come. That was something strange, because, according to the rules governing caravans for thousands of years, it was understood that the usual trails should never be departed from, and, further, it was understood that no one should trot at night. Also our Turkish guides thought they were robbers, as it was reported in Dschidda that a band of 40 thieves were roaming around. While at Lidd I sent information on ahead to the authorities at Dschidda and also at Mekka, so I was reasonably certain that the entire region between these points would know of our coming. Everybody would also know that we were not an

ordinary commercial caravan, accompanied merely by the
usual guard, but that our caravan consisted of 50 armed men
especially equipped with four machine guns. Therefore I had
not worried much about the 40 thieves roaming around here.
In order to be better able to control and protect my men, I
broke the long line of camels into two parts, making two lines
of 50 camels each. I forbade the usual sleeping aboard the
camels, had the guns prepared, and saw everything cleared for
action. The orders for my men were, no matter what happened, to "Gather around the leader!"

The officers rode at the head of the caravan. As the first
light of day appeared over the high mountains, rising up out
of the desert on our right hand, I began to believe that all
was well and that an attack by Bedouins in daylight was not
to be expected. I therefore hung my rifle over the saddle,
unstrapped my heavy cartridge belt and rode slowly along the
caravan to inspect the right flank.

I had arrived at the middle of the caravan when I suddenly
heard a clear, sharp whistle, followed by the crash of a volley.
A rain of lead fell uninterruptedly upon our caravan from all
sides and at short range. The whizzing and whistling of bullets was so loud and continuous that I was unable to make
myself heard sufficiently to give orders. I tore my gun off the
saddle, sprang to the ground and ran forward followed by my
men. At the head of the caravan the engagement had really
commenced. We could see the flashes of the enemy guns
through the twilight about 80 meters away. The riflemen
themselves could not be seen, nor could they see us much
better, while the tall forms of the camels were plainly visible,
forming excellent targets for the enemy. Our only points of
aim were the flashes of the enemy guns. As we were attacked
on all sides, it was impossible to decide which way to turn
next. The larger part of my men lay up forward with me. A
small part remained at the rear as per my orders. Then we
decided to bring our best weapons, the machine guns, into
action. Two of these were tied up on the camels up forward,

the other two at the rear. After a few moments the machine guns were brought into action, and hardly had they begun to rattle off their salvos over the enemy's line, when the enemy, not accustomed to this new form of attack, ceased firing. We made use of this pause to pull the still standing camels to the ground, so that they would not make such excellent targets, and then we issued out ammunition and consolidated our forces.

Having received the heaviest fire from forward and to the left, I brought my men up to that point. Our offensive equipment consisted of four machine guns, 13 German rifles, 10 old Turkish rifles that I received in Kunfidda to replace the ones lost out of the zambuk, and three modern Turkish rifles that were divided among the officers. In addition, we had 24 revolvers, but these could only be used for close action. I could not determine the exact strength of the enemy. There might have been 60 or 70 firing rapidly, or there might possibly have been considerably more firing leisurely. The question of enemy strength would soon be answered when the approaching daylight appeared. As it grew lighter we could see that all the nearest sand-hills, completely surrounding us, were black with Bedouins. My men behaved excellently. In spite of the overwhelming strength of the enemy, who were estimated at not less than 300, there was not the slightest sign of fear among any of my men. Although I had not given any orders, bayonets had been fixed on the muzzles of all the rifles. While I was considering what should next be done, the answer to my question came from a man lying close to me on my right hand, who said: "What next? Are we going to start soon, lieutenant?" "What do?" was my return question. "Why, charge them, of course!" replied this 18-year-old stripling. "So be it. You are right. Rise and charge!" And, amid loud cheers, we charged the enemy's line. Such a proceeding at a caravan-looting was certainly something new. Likewise very few shots came from the enemy. When the glittering bayonets came on, the enemy fled precipitously. Our fire, thinning out his ranks, followed him. First we charged to the left, then forward, and then to the right. It was unnecessary to charge the rear. They had already disappeared in that quarter.

In that way we widened the surrounding circle so that the enemy was now about 1200 meters away. The firing ceased. I assembled my men around the caravan. The machine guns remained in position all ready for instant use.

In spite of the rain of bullets, which they showered on us at almost point-blank range, we had, thank God, but one German wounded. But when I turned toward our Arabian allies I was dumbfounded. In Germany we have a proverb that says "He counts the number of his loved ones, and behold, instead of six he finds seven." But here this proverb was reversed. Of the 24 gendarmes there remained but seven. There were no deaths. The missing ones we found later on in Dschidda. The Arabs that stood by us had been hit in the legs. This was caused by their remaining behind seeking shelter among the camels instead of advancing on the enemy with us. As my men were firing from the ground at a distance of about 30 to 40 meters in advance of the camels, the enemy could not see them in the dark and fired over their heads. They could only see the large camels. Before it occurred to the Arabs to drag the camels down to earth and thereby be better protected, the enemy bullets flew between the camels' legs and struck the precious bodies of these heroes.

We knew nothing of course concerning the enemy's casualties. We did, however, count 15 dead ones in the places they abandoned when we charged. These corpses, except one, had neither rifles nor ammunition. According to Bedouin custom, the fallen are despoiled of their weapons. The single gun captured, a breech-loading rifle of modern English construction, was added to our service. We could still see the Bedouins on the sand-hills in the distance. As soon as any of them showed themselves, they were immediately fired upon, because it then occurred to me to give them a good moral lesson.

We could not remain in our present position very long. At

first I had an idea that I was confronted merely by an ordinary robbery, and imagined that the enemy, having already suffered a handsome loss, would see the error of his ways and accordingly disappear.

A large number of our camels were struck. We unstrapped all supplies from them that were of any value, especially the water, and placed them on the other camels instead of the less necessary equipment which we then left behind.

I decided to turn sharp to the left in the direction of the sea, which could be discerned shimmering in the distance. If I reached there I would have at least one flank free. It certainly angered me to be unable to use the machine guns on the march as I had no suitable gun carriages. They had to be carried on camels. In order to keep the caravan closely consolidated, I formed it in ranks of four to six camels. The wounded were secured to the sides of the camels away from the enemy so as to be better protected. Two camels with two machine guns rode out ahead, the other two machine guns were similarly carried at the rear; an advance guard of 10 men in open order preceded the caravan by about 150 meters, a rear guard of 10 men also marched the same distance in the rear. Nine men with rifles were disposed as best we could on the two flanks. The other men, armed solely with revolvers and who could, therefore, only fight at short range, remained in the middle of the caravan. The advance guard was commanded by Lieutenant Gerdis, the rear guard by Lieutenant Schmidt, the flanks by Lieutenant Gyszling. The caravan itself, with Dr. Lang in charge of the wounded, was led by Lieutenant Wellmann.

Slowly we got underway; flags waving at the head. My hopes that the enemy would not further molest us were not fulfilled. After marching about 10 minutes we were fired on again from all sides. We could hardly see the enemy. The sand-hills prevented our looking ahead further than 400 meters. We could only see about 10 or 20 black heads bob up on this sand-hill and then on that sand-hill. The next instant a salvo would fall around the caravan, and before we could prepare to return the fire the heads would disappear and another hail of lead would come from a different direction.

Most remarkably, we had no casualties at first, even though the enemy's fire was heavy, small sand splashes rising about us, while pebbles and sand flecks flew up into our faces. Soon we discovered that the heaviest attack was directed on the rear guard. Every few minutes the men there had to turn about and, by heavy firing, check the enemy.

I was with the rear guard when I received word from forward that strong detachments of the enemy were forming ahead of us. On arrival at the advance guard I found the whole horizon black with Bedouins. At the same time I received word from aft that one of the camels carrying a machine gun was shot down. The rear guard stopped to cover the machine gun and Lieutenant Schmidt ordered another camel unloaded and sent to the rear. I had already heard the machine guns of the rear guard firing. They had, in the meantime, been unstrapped and run into action.

I then brought the caravan to a halt, which was not an easy matter as the majority of the Arabian gendarmes and camel drivers had deserted into the night at the beginning of the fight. On my way to the rear guard I received word that a seaman, Rademacher by name, had been killed and that Lieutenant Schmidt was fatally wounded by bullets through his abdomen and breast. Lieutenant Wellmann had by this time assumed command of the rear guard, bringing with him from the caravan two animals to carry the machine guns.

As we waited, the enemy's fire again increased and soon we were in the midst of a lively engagement. Suddenly, as if by magic, the firing absolutely ceased, and as I dumfoundedly looked around for the reason, I saw two of the still remaining Arabian gendarmes waving large white cloths and running toward the enemy. At the same time a third Arabian gendarme came to me to explain that his comrades wished to hold a parley with the enemy. As unnecessary as I deemed this to be, it was from the first wholly pleasing, because I had in the meantime clearly seen that this was not an ordinary robbery, but that we actually faced an organized military situation. As we were outnumbered at least ten to one, a march with camels on the open level under the continuous fire of the enemy was impossible. My most powerful weapons, the machine guns, could not be used on the march, and my 29 rifles were not much protection as I had an insufficient number of men to use them on all sides at the same time. And finally we would gradually be picked off one after the other as we proceeded.

We used the pause in the firing to intrench ourselves. We made breastworks out of camel saddles (filled with sand), coffee, rice and provision sacks. The encircling walls we filled up, to the best of our ability, with sand. In the middle of the camp we gathered the camels. Loop-holes were made in great haste. Other facilities lacking, we made the loop-holes with our swords, and tin plates (scoops). Of course, our construction work was done so hurriedly that it was not as efficient as could be desired. We buried the water containers deep in the sand so that the enemy bullets would not rip them open and thus inflict irreparable damage. In the middle of the camp we constructed another small protection out of sand-filled petroleum tins, the walls being about $1\frac{1}{2}$ meters thick. Within this we placed the disabled and sick men, the wounded and the doctor.

As we could expect to be attacked from all sides, and as our breastworks protected us only from the front, we so placed the camels around the sides that we also had "living" protection from the rear. Lieutenant Schmidt, fatally wounded, was carried into the camp on a stretcher made of rifles and woolen blankets. The dead seaman was buried then and there.

The four machine guns were planted at the corners, each hastily protected by a hurriedly thrown up sand-hill. The riflemen were detailed around to the important points, the men armed with revolvers were shoved into the gaps, and ammunition served out. We had hardly finished these preparations when the enemy's terms (stipulations) arrived. They were:

"Deliver all weapons and ammunition, all camels, all provisions and water, and pay £11,000 in gold. We could then proceed unmolested." Now what do you think of that!

The negotiations were started by the dragoman, who, with his wife, had joined us at Kunfidda. He also was wounded! Shot in the legs! When he went out to parley, he did not forget to take his wife along. The next time we saw them was in Dschidda.

The answer that I gave, declared:

"In the first place we had no money. In the second place we were guests of the land. Get your gold in Dschidda. In the third place it is not a German custom to deliver up our arms."

And then the firing recommenced. The remaining camel drivers and a number of the Arabian gendarmes improved their time so well during the pause that they followed our interpreter and his wife and also disappeared. The fighting continued until dark. Lying there between our camels and their saddles, we were fairly well protected. I ordered that their fire be returned slowly. We did not have a great quantity of ammunition and we found many cartridges that failed to fire owing to their having been submerged overnight when the zambuk capsized. Therefore I saved all the best ammunition for the machine guns so that in case of a night attack I could count on my most powerful weapons for a fight at close quarters. The remaining ammunition was divided among the riflemen. We had no further casualties. A number of camels were shot, but that did not lessen our protection. A dead camel holds just as many bullets as a live one. The whole day, however, we did not eat. We had no time to think of that during daylight. No sooner would one of our men poke his head over the saddles than a heavy fire was showered on us.

The principal work started at nightfall. About one hour after sunset the moon rose. During this hour it was so dark that we could hardly see more than 40 or 50 meters. Everything in the camp was cleared for repelling an attack in case they stormed us. All rifles and pistols were loaded, and machine guns made ready for instant use, the men kneeling with their guns resting on the breastworks. But nothing happened. With the rising of the moon we could see about 300 meters and then we set to work to improve our camp. First we issued out water and passed around some hardtack. A part of the officers and men remained on watch and ready. The others continued to dig the trenches deeper, a job which proceeded very slowly because of the lack of proper tools. The dead camels had to be gotten rid of. The carcasses decayed very rapidly in the extreme heat. They swelled up, the skin burst (along the welts caused by whipping) leaving the entrails exposed.

It was long into the night before our work had progressed sufficiently so that we could no longer begrudge ourselves a little rest. The trenches were now deep enough to afford sufficient protection to a man lying down. On all sides, outboard of the camels, we built sand-hills. The rifles and revolvers were so choked with sand that they had to be taken apart, cleaned and then proof fired. Then we bound up the breech mechanisms with our handkerchiefs and placed small rag wads in the muzzles in order to keep out the sand. Above all things, the weapons had to be protected. In camp we kept a sort of watch in that a certain portion of men remained on post. The remainder were allowed to sleep on their loaded arms. One officer was always on watch. During the night the enemy did not attempt anything startling.

At 9 P.M. Lieutenant Schmidt, who had been fatally wounded, died. We dug a deep grave in the middle of the camp and about 11 P.M. we four officers carried our comrade to his last resting place. The funeral had to be conducted without the honors of volley firing. This honor was paid our dead on the next day by the enemy.

As Dschidda was only 10 hours away by camel and eight hours on foot, I sent, during the hour preceding moonlight, an English-speaking Arab that I had brought from Hodeida, into the town. The man had always appeared to be sensible and reliable. As I learned later, he was able to steal through the enemy lines and to carry the information about our camp to the military authorities at Dschidda.

A half hour before sunrise I had all hands awakened. This in case the enemy was there and waiting to recommence the fighting as early as possible. I intended, in order to make a moral impression, to immediately answer his first shots with heavy salvos so that he would know that we were all on watch and that our strength had not diminished.

My expectations were realized. At sunrise the enemy opened a heavy fire. We answered immediately, energetically firing full salvos, and each head that was exposed was soon covered by our fire. This proceeding as we could see, lowered the morale of the enemy. His firing grew markedly more cautious and weak. We had therefore accomplished our purpose.

Prior to sunrise, each man was given a glass of water. For the remainder of the day I could not let them have any more. Not until after sunset was it possible to take another drink. As we could not cook during the night, the hardtack were eagerly eaten and pockets were stuffed full of them.

The enemy fired in a desultory manner. As we were very well protected, we gave only a weak reply. That we were not dealing with an ordinary robbery, but with an organized force instead, was presently clearly made known to us. From our camp we could see two large zambuks at anchor off the coast. A regular transportation service was being conducted between the zambuks and our besiegers. No doubt most of our enemies arrived there in these two ships. Another part came from overland because we could see a great horde of camels grazing along the desert horizon.

Unfortunately we had two more severely wounded that day. Of these, a fireman, Lanig by name, shot through the breast and stomach, died during the night. We could not give our wounded much medical assistance, as we had lost all our medical outfit when the zambuk sank. Luckily we still had some of the *Emden*'s first-aid packages (that is, rolls of medicated bandages) and several bottles of cognac.

The day was uneventful. We were made uncomfortable, however, because one of the camels which broke out of the camp was shot to windward and the wind carried the most penetrating and putrid odors toward us. In the camp itself we were pestered by some most unwelcome guests. Hundreds of thousands of disgusting black beetles, about as long as one's thumb, ran right and left over the whole camp carrying camel manure. Our trenches were full of these animals and no matter how many one killed or trod on there were always more coming. Sleeping was practically out of the question. They crawled in through your clothes and walked out over your face. Moreover, in addition to being extremely unpleasant they introduced an immediate danger to our wounded; tetanus germs breed more quickly in horse and camel manure than in anything else. Such an infection is always followed by the absolutely deadly lockjaw.

The glowing sun made living in the daytime almost unbearable. Our light-colored head-dress could not be worn as it furnished the enemy a fine point of aim, while the dazzling light caused smarting eyes and headaches. It was so hot that one's hands were burned while shooting if the barrel of the gun were touched. The grease-soaked camel saddles began to swell, due to the heat, and the ensuing smoky odor constantly pervaded the camp. We covered the saddles with sand as best we could. The wind never ceased blowing fine particles of sand all over us. Meantime we had to dig out the trenches again because they became half filled with sand. The fine sand particles entered the eyes, ears, mouth and nose. The eyes burned from this continuous irritation. A heavy sand coat, made by the perspiration, covered our faces so as to make us unrecognizable. About 20 to 30 vultures circled high in the air above the camp.

At sunset the regular preparations were made again. Two

Arabian gendarmes, disguised as Bedouins, were sent as messengers this night to Dschidda. When the moon rose the men not on watch lay down to sleep. The enemy began to fire when night fell.

In the middle of the night our sentries began to shoot. Everything was ready for action, standing by to repulse the expected attack. "Where are they?" I asked the sentry. "Here, there were several crawling around about 40 meters away." And then a shower of lead was fired at them. Our guess that these were enemies was a mistake. They were hyenas and jackals that had crept up around the camp looking for prey and found the camels' carcasses to feast on.

And now the sun rose for the third time over our camp. Our situation was critical. We had received no signs as yet from the Turkish garrison that our messengers had arrived, as they should have done, the preceding day. We could hold out this one day and then the water would be gone in spite of the fact that each man received only one small cup of water each morning and evening. Without water we were lost. We had to do something before our men lost their strength. So I gave the order that morning that we would make a powerful attempt to break through to Dschidda at sunset unless some news came in the course of the day. I had hoped thereby to get at least some part of my men through. Whoever fell, fell. The sick and wounded could nott be taken along. We hoped to God that such extreme measures would not have to be adopted.

About noon on the third day, a man waving a white cloth suddenly appeared from that side where the firing had ceased. I admitted him to the camp and asked what he wanted. He answered that the enemy had abandoned the idea of our delivering up our arms, munitions, camels, provisions and water. Instead we should pay £22,000 in gold. I guessed that the enemy had information that the Turkish garrison was coming out and that now, as is customary with these people, they were endeavoring, as a last resort, to get as much out of us as they possibly could. I therefore decided to draw out the proceedings as long as practicable, to ward off the raising of the siege, and then to bring the enemy between two fires. Therefore I painted a rosy description of our camp and pretended that nothing could be more agreeable to us than to spend the fresh summer in the desert, the music of salvo firing being very pleasant. I showed the man the place where our empty water containers were buried and made it clear to him that with that amount of water I could comfortably hold out four weeks longer, and therefore I knew no reason why I should agree to any disadvantageous terms. Munitions I had in abundance, as he knew. They could thank their lucky stars that I hadn't turned my machine guns loose on them and pressed the attack home. The parley was held through a Moroccan, who had been taken prisoner in Belgium and was sent back from there along with the other Mohammedans to Turkey. He had accompanied an expedition into Arabia, was picked up by me in Kunfidda and still remained with us. He spoke a little broken French.

The enemy's emissary did not seem to be much impressed with my explanation. He left, but returned in another half hour and offered the same terms. In order to gain time I told him that I preferred above all to do business with the enemy commander in person, and invited the commander himself to visit me in my camp. The suspicious angel came not, but instead sent me the terrible threat that since we refused to pay, we would now have *beaucoup de combat*. I took this to mean that it was high time for him to leave and I expressed my surprise that their previous actions should also not be classed as *beaucoup de combat*.

To me it had seemed so. Then we received some furious and violent salvos. Following this a dead silence ensued.

A quarter and then a half hour passed without a single shot. Slowly and carefully we raised our heads over the camel saddles. Nothing in sight. "Be careful," I said, "that is only a ruse. Keep under cover! We have plenty of time. We can't

leave before evening anyway." But as nothing further happened we began to get up, first on our knees, then finally we
stood up and searched with our glasses. Nothing in sight. We
knew not where they had disappeared. The sand-hills of the
desert that swallowed them up now cut off our view. Evidently they had withdrawn.

The next thing to do was to remain lying, because I was
not yet certain the enemy had really retreated or whether he
was trying to fool us. Anyway, we could not possibly proceed
before night.

About an hour after the firing ceased two camel riders appeared, who, from their clothes and rich saddle cloths, were
recognized as belonging to a class above the Bedouins. Waving a white cloth they rode up to our camp. We hoisted up
our battle-flag as a sign that we had seen them. They rode up
to within 50 meters and then dismounted. I sent my Moroccan out to them to find out what they wanted. The answer
came back that they wished to speak to the commander of the
German troops. They came from the Emir of Mecca, who had
heard of the attack made on us and was sending troops to our
aid.

That sounded pretty good, but there appeared no signs that
this was really true. I had grown sufficiently accustomed to
Arabia to be rather distrustful. I went out to them with my
bared saber in my hand; behind me marched one of my men
with his gun ready. I gave orders in the camp to be ready for
an attack, and in case of any attack on me to commence firing
regardless of my personal safety. But nothing occurred. The
two men declared to me that the second son of the Emir of
Mecca, Abdullah, would soon ride up with his troop. Correct,
a half hour later a caravan of 70 camel riders appeared on the
horizon carrying a dark red banner on which were inscribed
various Koran characters. They made some sort of music on
their drums and sang to it. This proceeding I thought to be
rather imprudent as the troops were supposed to be ready to
go into battle.

Abdullah approached to greet me. He conveyed the compliments of his father, spoke his regrets at our having been attacked and said that he had water for us; we could now quietly proceed to Dschidda, as our enemies had retreated.

I distributed the water among my men, then under great difficulties packed the camels, a job which is not an easy one as "getting a camel ready" had not heretofore been described in the *Bluejacket's Manual* of the navy. A large amount of provisions had to be left behind because about 40 of our camels had been shot. Accompanied by the emir's troops, we left the camp. It is certainly a rare occurrence to see a Christian riding in the desert under the flag of the prophet, next to the son of the Emir of Mecca. After a few minutes we passed over the abandoned lines of the enemy. The scoundrels had actually built themselves perfectly good trenches.

We rode the whole of the next day and then encamped at a well. Here, for the first time in four days, we were able to have cooked food, to wash and to lie down to rest. The well was probably supplied with water by a spring and was about 40 meters deep. The water that we drew from this well was warm, probably about 30° Celsius.

From our camp, close to the edge of the sea, we could see a restless searchlight sweeping through the darkness. Our friends, the English, before Dschidda!

CHAPTER 20

To the Railroad

WE WERE VERY COMFORTABLY quartered in Dschidda. The sick and wounded were given good treatment in a military hospital. It was hard to decide which way to continue my journey. I was told that the Bedouins who had attacked us were paid to do so by the English; and they were armed with the most modern English rifles. Leaving here by water was next to impossible. The numerous tips of the masts of the English blockading fleet were visible daily. In spite of that I decided to leave in zambuks. I still continued to believe that the sea routes contained greater possibilities than the land routes.

Therefore it now became necessary to spread the rumor that I expected to proceed overland. Secretly, however, I procured a zambuk and a reliable pilot. I was forced to remain in Dschidda several days because of the wounded. The departure date was set for April 8. I used a small motorboat, which I discovered in Dschidda harbor, to make a reconnaissance out to sea for a considerable distance. I saw no English. Was it possible that they actually swallowed the rumor about the overland route!

Having found a favorable breeze during the night of April 8–9, we started out. Conditions were much more favorable than when we broke through the English blockade off Hodeida. The wind held through the night and by sunrise we were out of sight of the blockading English. I kept the zambuk as near the beach as possible, squeezing closely to all the reefs in order to render pursuit more difficult. Slowly, but surely, we made headway. We stopped for a short time, not more than a few hours, at several small coast towns in order to get the latest small coast towns in order to get the latest information and to purchase fresh provisions. The pilot I carried from Dschidda knew the coast very well and, in addition, spoke fairly good English. We anchored at night because we dared not sail through the reefs in the dark. At Scherm, Rabegh, I changed zambuks. The one I brought from Dschidda was very frail. We had to fill the new zambuk with sand ballast. Without either cargo or sand ballast, it was not very safe to sail her.

The evening anchoring was invariably an unusual evolution. We could not anchor wherever we wished. The coral reefs, among which we sailed, were surrounded by great depths of water. We anchored in something like the following manner. Sailing up to within a few meters of the reef we would douse sail. Two Arabs were standing on the bow ready to jump overboard, carrying with them a small line with iron grapnel hooks on it. These hooks were jammed in the cavities under the blocks of coral that were found near the surface. And so we lay. This was not always practicable, however, because in case the wind shifted we would have been set on the coral bank and stuck fast.

We encountered a few sailing ships approaching from the north. It is an Arabian custom for two ships, when meeting, to greet each other with "howling." The passing ships were somewhat surprised to hear our 50 strong throats chiming in with the energetic howling of their native associates of our zambuk.

There are no coast clans along this entire stretch, but we did encounter out at sea some small dugouts containing Arabians engaged in fishing; and on those occasions we substituted fish for rice on our menu.

Along the way northward we passed Mecca. The Arabians, as is their custom, carried on their prayers five times each day facing toward their holy city, bumping their foreheads on the ground. And so it happened that in the first days they faced forward when praying, later on they faced to starboard, and finally they faced aft.

Encountering no unusual difficulties we reached (April 28) Scherm Mannaiburra, a small protected harbor about 10 miles south of "El Weg," our goal. From there on we had to proceed without the protection of reefs, deep water being found close up to the beach. We had succeeded in hewing our way through for approximately the past six months, so it was now up to us to avoid every possible danger on this last stretch which was still dangerous. So I decided not to sail this distance, but to anchor off Scherm Munnaiburra and proceed overland to El Weg.

The authorities there had been previously notified of our coming by messengers who had gone overland. Several gendarmes had been sent out along the coast to meet us. One of these we picked up at our anchorage and sent him ahead to provide camels. During the night we could see small signal fires on the beach which showed us that our caravan had already been assembled. We took our guns and only sufficient provisions for one day. The remainder we sent back, with our compliments, on the zambuk. Luckily, this zambuk also managed to return home without sighting an enemy ship. We arrived at El Weg in the evening of April 29.

The first thing we did here was to get thoroughly rested, also thoroughly bathed. Here, also, we finally secured another opportunity of having our clothes washed and changed. It took two days to prepare the caravan.

About 8 A.M., May 2, we marched out. In the north camels

are ridden differently than they are ridden in the south. Down south, as we well knew, the camels are secured one behind the other in a long row, while up here in the north this is not customary. Each animal is ridden singly and must therefore be steered by its own rider. This was difficult at first, but after a while my men grew accustomed to it and managed to keep their beasts in hand, so that the caravan kept together after a fashion. We were guided by the Sheik Suleiman from El Weg.

At first we marched through the desert, sufficiently familiar to us. But soon we came to a beautiful region. We went through the mountains amid wonderful scenery. The water supply also was much better than on our previous desert journeys. The wells were more numerous, supplying drinkable, even though not quite clean, water. Our Arabian guides had told us several days before that we should be greatly surprised when we saw running water on the top of the mountain. We did find the rivulet and it was actually flowing, but the whole thing could be stopped by a man placing both feet across the channel. As it was quite cool, we marched in the mountains during daylight and slept by night.

As we had heretofore experienced so much danger in the desert, we intrenched ourselves each night, to the bewilderment of the Arabian guides. But we had finally reached the conclusion that no one was to be trusted. The intrenching did not take long because we had now provided ourselves with shovels. And so each evening we built a small armed camp in the desert from which pointed four threatening machine guns. We made no watch fires in the middle of the camp, but the sentries on outposts that circled the camp built fires which made sufficient illumination. As usual, we slept on our loaded arms. A camp such as this was not what you might call comfortable. The nights were very cold. Most of us had to give up our blankets to the sick men. But those that had no blankets did not complain, but simply followed the old rule, *i.e.,* "Lie on your back and cover yourself with your stomach."

The territory of our guide, Suleiman Pascha, did not quite reach to El Ula, where we would arrive at the Hedschas Railroad. Close to El Ula we would come into the territory of some other sheik who was not on good terms with our friends, so I could not use his camels on the last four hours of the trip through the other sheik's territory. Under these circumstances it appeared as if we would have to make another strenuous "breaking-through" attempt. Suleiman Pascha also expected something of the sort. During the course of the day all the sheik's adherents from the surrounding mountains joined him in small bodies, until the caravan finally reached a total strength of about 400 men. They certainly did make a most picturesque sight with their long Arabian guns, flowing brown robes and fluttering head-cloths. Although previously to this we had intrenched for our own protection, now Suleiman Pascha himself adopted similar protective measures for his men. A sign that conditions here were rather unsettled. We ourselves made similar detailed preparations. But the night passed quietly.

Now we were only one day's journey from the railroad station. Our trail led through high mountains. There were some narrow passes to go through which seemed to have been especially built for making a surprise attack. Only one camel at a time could pass along so the caravan had to be strung out in a very long line and could not be maneuvered as a unit. In order to avoid a surprise, Suleiman organized a regular reconnoitering force which was wonderful to behold. Possibly this excellent reconnaissance was due to no little practice along that line in the past. Small patrols galloped ahead into each valley, collected information and raced back again to inform the main caravan. They reported that the wicked sheik of the next territory was, for the present, engaged in a raid to the northward, so we could proceed unmolested.

When I heard this news I decided to ride on ahead of the caravan in order to get on the wire at El Ula as soon as possible in order to provide for a special train and make the necessary preparations for the accommodations for my men. A few hours of trotting took me out of the territory of Suleiman Pascha, his two sons and the various other worthies. We made good friends with the sheik and his two sons, even though we could not thoroughly understand each other. The greatest interest was aroused among all three when, as we came through a mountain pass and could see the distant houses of El Ula among the palms, I took out my binoculars and endeavored to once more find a trace of a railroad line or a telegraph wire. Binoculars had never been heard of before in this country. Each wanted to see through them so the glasses were passed from hand to hand, each one continuing to turn the focussing arrangement a little more. What the last one managed to see was a mystery to me. In order to impress the accompanying Arabs with the power of our weapons, I fired a short string from a machine gun, much to the astonishment of Suleiman Pascha. He did not dare to turn his head, and was much pleased when I brought down a continuous stream of stones from the cliffs at which I was aiming. As all Arabs are exceedingly interested in firearms, I gave the Pascha and his two sons each a revolver and some ammunition and I promised to send him a pair of binoculars from Germany.

As we were passing along a very high plain whose limits could hardly be seen, I used this occasion to impress the sheik with the might of Germany. He was very astonished when I told him that a German ship could bring the enemy under fire even at a range much greater than the distance across this plain. Although this was a bit overdrawn, as the plain reached from one horizon to the other, it nevertheless created the desired impression. In regard to the size of the guns, I told him that a camel could comfortably gallop through inside of one.

I reached El Ula about noon and to my surprise found everything already prepared. A special train awaited us, the engine being all ready for the order to light fires. And this order was speedily given. Two German gentlemen and a number of Turkish officers had come way down there to meet us, bringing us letters and information, and, from the German Colony in Syria, presents of cold Rhine wine, Sekt, pears and such other tasty bits which we had not had in a long time. When I first had to choose between bathing or drinking wine, I chose the latter. Why suddenly break off our pleasant habits after remaining true to them for weeks at a time?

A few hours later my men also rode in.

I rode out a piece to meet them, and, while being photographed from all sides, with flying flags we made our entry into this small town whose railroad line and waiting room gave us our first sight of real evidences of civilization. Wonderful food, very wonderful drinks, a short bath (of course) took up the next few hours. Then the train started north at the unheard of speed of 30 kilometers per hour, while we gave ourselves up to the long lost luxury of stretching out our weary bones on the red cushions.

CHAPTER 21

Homeward Bound

Dᵁᴿᴵᴺᴳ ᴛʜᴇ ʀᴇᴍᴀᴵᴺᴅᴇʀ ᴏғ the journey we anticipated no further dangers. We travelled by rail via Damascus and Aleppo through Asia Minor toward Constantinople. At two places we had to leave the train and proceed in wagons and afoot, as the line is not completed clear through.

In the most hospitable and whole-souled manner we were everywhere received by the German population and by the Turkish authorities. At every depot we found large crowds of people to greet us. We were received with music and waving flags and decorated with roses. Gifts were showered into our cars. We were provided with complete new outfits of clothing, and without tears we discarded our old rags and their millions of co-inhabitants. My men, who had heretofore not been accorded such an unusual distinction, were invited to sit at the same table with the exalted functionaries and high civil authorities. Many priceless gifts were presented to us, and our baggage car, which had contained only our munitions and our old rags, gradually began to fill up. At the sidings, which were especially operated so as not to inconvenience us, large swarms of Bedouins gathered, raced along beside our cars and, whenever the train stopped, entertained us with trick riding. Many a good glass was drained in the family circles of the German residents.

Finally, at Aleppo, after 10 months of waiting, we received the first news from home. Letters from our loved ones and the Iron Cross—what more could be expected? We received two large sacks of mail so that we passed the next few days in reading the letters from home, in studying over the many letters and tales sent forward to us, in sending signatures [evidently post cards] and in consuming the supplies of cigars, chocolate, etc., contained among our presents.

On Whitsunday, in the afternoon, our train arrived at the station at Haidar-Pascha, the last Asiatic station on this railroad. My men had received the long looked-for uniforms which had been sent out, and the officers were also able to fit themselves out in accordance with European "Kultur," to whose arms we were again returning.

The chief of the Mediterranean fleet and, at the same time, chief of the Turkish fleet, Admiral Souchon, could not be dissuaded from coming with his staff clear to Haidar-Pascha to meet us. My men formed hurriedly. Our flag, that would no longer wave over us for 10 more months, was on the right wing. A few short commands which were smartly obeyed showed that even months of a life of privateering could not stamp out their military bearing; then I lowered the tip of my sword before my superior:

"I respectfully report the return of the *Emden*'s landing force consisting of five officers, seven petty officers and 37 men!"

Another Emden *Hero Returns Home*
THE ADVENTURES OF LIEUTENANT LAUTERBACH
(NAVAL RESERVE) DURING THE PAST YEAR[1]

Mr. Edward Lyell Fox, the noted American writer, whose book "Behind the Scenes in War-Ridden Germany" was of so much assistance in explaining our position to his countrymen, was granted the privilege of meeting Captain Lauterbach at the conclusion of his long journey, and to him he gave the following account, quoted verbatim, of his varied experiences:

"And so you would like to hear the story that escaped the reporters in San Francisco," began Captain Lauterbach, with a pleasant chuckle as a smile spread over his weather-beaten but still peculiarly young face. "Well, it was not as extraordinary as all that—you know, at that time when the *Emden* put the finishing touches on a Russian and a French ship—I have still lived through other things. But as Captain von Mueller knew that the Australian cruiser *Sydney* was on his trail and that we would sooner or later come to blows with her, he told me that I could not take part in this next engagement. I had taken part in the last fight, he said, and therefore would now have to make a place for another. The captain of our accompanying collier had also made an urgent request to be permitted to be present during a fight. And so there was nothing else for me to say.

"At Keeling, with a boatswain's mate and a machinist, I had to shift over to the collier, whose captain was then transferred to the *Emden*. It was known that Captain von Mueller intended to send Lieutenant von Mücke ashore to destroy the radio and cable stations on one of the Keeling Islands. We were told to cruise in the neighborhood and wait for the *Em-*

1. TRANSLATOR'S NOTE.—While translating the foregoing adventures of Lieutenant von Mücke, I found the following article in the German press, "Der Tag" (The Day), of Berlin, dated October 17, 1915. In the hopes that it would be of interest in connection with the *Ayesha* yarn, the translation is appended herewith.

den. In case she did not again appear, I was to open the sealed orders which had been given me. We hated to leave the *Emden* and could hardly take our eyes off her. We waited a day, then another, three, five, ten days, two weeks, but no signs of our *Emden*. Had something gone amiss? But—nonsense! Our *Emden*—nothing could happen to her. Some day we would see her smoke clouds on the horizon. And so four weeks passed. This uncertainty was unbearable, but the certainty, gradually becoming more apparent, that the *Emden* was destroyed, made the coldest blood boil in our veins. But, you know of course, that the *Emden* in her final fight filled the whole world with her fame. . . .

"Our supply of provisions was almost exhausted and we had nothing but rice and potatoes to live on. It is indeed a hard task to actually believe that a loving friend has passed away! At the end of the fifth week there seemed no use in hoping for the return of our cruiser. I cannot express to you the deep sorrow with which we had to accept her loss. I opened the secret orders. They directed me to proceed to the neutral Dutch harbor of Padang on the east coast of Sumatra. Imagine our bad luck! Just 24 hours before our arrival, the North German Lloyd steamer *Choising* had left Padang and later took aboard at sea, from the *Ayesha*, Lieutenant von Mücke and his party. As you know, Captain von Mücke had, several days previously, entered Padang in the renowned *Ayesha*, which was later on destroyed when they shifted to the *Choising*. Of course, I did not know all this until a long time afterward. Here I lay before the high mountains of this silly country of Padang and knew not how to find my way through this channel, swarming with islands, into the harbor. My charts were of little help because the positions of the dangerous rocks, water now washing over them, were not marked. I did not trust to luck to get in the harbor, but took special precautions to keep inside the three-mile limit where an enemy ship could not attack me without violating Dutch neutrality. From out there I signalled for a pilot. And then a huge ship appeared, heading in. A Dutchman I thought. But she then hoisted the English colors and I could read the name on her side, *Empress of Japan*. She came smoking up—as big as a mountain in comparison with our small collier. 'Stop!' she signalled. Had I disobeyed the order, she would have rammed me. She lowered a boat and an officer came aboard declaring me and my crew to be prisoners of war. My ship would be sunk.

"Before my eyes they sank the collier. My crew and I were taken as prisoners to Singapore. The natives of this island city were very friendly toward us. I had soon gained their confidence sufficiently to know that an attempt to escape would not miscarry. But I wanted to make preparations to take my crew with me when I fled. We then began to dig a tunnel under the wire fence that surrounded our prison-camp. We had scarcely completed our work when the famous revolution among the natives in Singapore broke out. The English blamed me for inciting the blacks against them. I herewith declare that this blame is founded on untruths. When the revolution had been settled, we completed our tunnel, and, during the following night, nine of us gained our freedom. We marched the entire night along the northwest coast. As we had $2000 among us, we were soon able to get hold of two Malayan rowboats which took us across the Straits to the Dutch Island. Here we found some more sea-faring Malayans who were glad to take us for a cruise of several days further along the east coast of Sumatra. But even here, in spite of the hospitality of the natives, we could not linger long because we dared not violate the Dutch rules. After a long trip through blooming tobacco fields and coffee plantations, through shady woods of rubber trees and endless plains covered with ylang-ylang, we managed to get through the almost impenetrable forest of the marshy coast regions, and finally arrived at the green Sea of Sumatra, where Malay seamen again awaited us to carry us across to Java and Celebes.

"A fairly large boat had been lying on the beach of Celebes

for the past seven months. It was an unreliable old thing that absorbed more water than a thirsty sailor could, even with his advantage of being able to drink more freely. But we took a chance and, in high spirits, stood out into the Sulu Sea. We had nothing to steer by except a pocket compass. During the night we consumed great quantities of matches trying to keep on the course. This was set for the Philippine Islands. How we managed to get safely over the Sulu Sea, God only knows! The boat danced like a nut-shell on the heavy seas.

"Land! On the seventh day out of Celebes we sighted land. We certainly did learn to sympathize with old Columbus and his experiences in his day. It was Mindanao, the land of the black Moros, that now took us up as guests. Particularly the Americans living out there showed themselves to be very friendly. As our skins had peeled off and as we were burned to a dark brown, it was difficult to believe that we were really of European origin. Therefore we were considerably alarmed to hear the news that six Moros had gone "amuk" and were roaming the country, trying to kill off all the whites. It was later declared that they were last seen in the same direction in the jungles through which we would have to pass in order to reach the north coast. This was not a pleasant prospect inasmuch as we were armed with nothing but pocket knives. We kept watch day and night until we reached our goal where we expected to meet our small steamer. Of course, it was not there. We therefore set forth in a small sailboat for the island of Cebu, and from there we finally reached Manila.

"Here I shipped aboard the Japanese steamer *Takachi Maru* for Tientsin. I told the grinning skipper that I was a Hollander. But he did not seem to trust my nationality and continually spoke to me in English. 'Cannot understand; only Dutch!' But this he did not understand. I was afraid of being recognized in Shanghai, as I had frequently entered that port as captain of a Hamburg-American liner, so I therefore cut off my beard and mustache. As quickly as possible I turned my back on Shanghai and, with two donkeys drawing my ancient Chinese wagon, proceeded into the interior where I was concealed by a friend. Eventually I heard that an American steamer, the *Mongolia,* would proceed from Shanghai to Japan. I therefore returned to Shanghai to make proper preparations. During the night on which the *Mongolia* was to sail I went aboard and reserved a cabin. Three days later, after no adventures, I landed in Japan. Unconcernedly and without molestation, I wandered around the country of our yellow enemies for eight days. Then I booked passage for America via Honolulu. And there on board I was recognized by a gentleman who had once upon a time been a passenger on one of my Hamburg ships.

"In sufficient time I heard that the reporters and photographers of San Francisco would be waiting for me. These were the very people whom I wished above all things to avoid. They did not catch me."

In regard to the last part of his trip, Captain Lauterbach had little to say. He merely requested Mr. Fox to warn his countrymen about the horrible proceedings going on in the dives disguised as whiskey stores along the New York waterfront. A refugee these days must travel by devious paths if he wishes to arrive home safely and unrecognized.

Captain Lauterbach then wrote a postcard. I volunteered to mail the letter for him. "That is addressed to an acquaintance," he said, laughing up his sleeve. "He bet me two hundred pounds that I would never return home to Germany. He loses."

CLASSICS OF NAVAL LITERATURE
JACK SWEETMAN, SERIES EDITOR

Ned Myers; or, A Life Before the Mast, by James Fenimore Cooper. Introduction and notes by William S. Dudley

The Quiet Warrior: A Biography of Admiral Raymond A. Spruance, by Thomas B. Buell. Introduction by John B. Lundstrom

Raiders of the Deep, by Lowell Thomas. Introduction and notes by Gary E. Weir

Recollections of a Naval Officer, 1841–1865, by Capt. William Harwar Parker. Introduction and notes by Craig L. Symonds

The Riddle of the Sands, by Erskine Childers. Introduction and notes by Eric Grove

The Rise of American Naval Power, 1775–1918, by Harold and Margaret Sprout. Introduction by Kenneth J. Hagan and Charles Conrad Campbell

Running the Blockade, by Thomas E. Taylor. Introduction and notes by Stephen R. Wise

Run Silent, Run Deep, by Edward L. Beach. Introduction by Edward P. Stafford

Sailor of Fortune: The Life and Adventures of Commodore Barney, USN, by Hulbert Footner. Introduction by Geoffrey Footner

A Sailor of King George: The Journals of Captain Frederick Hoffman, RN, 1793–1814, edited by A. Beckford Bevan and H. B. Wolryche-Whitmore. Introduction, notes, and glossary by Gerald Jordan

A Sailor's Log, by Robley D. Evans. Introduction and notes by Benjamin Franklin Cooling

Samurai! by Saburo Sakai with Martin Caidin and Fred Saito. Introduction by Barrett Tillman

The Sand Pebbles, by Richard McKenna. Introduction by Robert Shenk

Sea Devils: Italian Navy Commandos in World War II, by J. Valerio Borghese. Introduction by Paolo E. Coletta

The Sinking of the Merrimac, by Richmond Pearson Hobson. Introduction and notes by Richard W. Turk

Stoddert's War: Naval Operations during the Quasi-War with France, 1798–1801, by Michael A. Palmer. New introduction by the author

A Voice from the Main Deck: Being a Record of the Thirty Years' Adventures of Samuel Leech. Introduction and notes by Michael J. Crawford